KU-759-321

Ella's kitchen

the Cook Book

For Ella and Paddy who inspire us every day. And for all of their generation — may good food bring joy throughout your lives.

Paul + Alison Lindley

An Hachette UK Company
www.hachette.co.uk

First published in Great Britain in 2013 by Hamlyn, an imprint of Octopus Publishing Group Ltd
Carmelite House
50 Victoria Embankment
London EC4Y 0DZ
www.octopusbooks.co.uk

Revised edition 2019

Copyright © Octopus Publishing Group Ltd 2013, 2019
Text copyright © Ella's Kitchen (Brands) Limited 2013, 2019
Photography copyright © Octopus Publishing Group Ltd 2013, 2019
Illustrations copyright © Ella's Kitchen (Brands) Limited 2013, 2019

Ella's Kitchen is a subsidiary of The Hain Celestial Group.

All rights reserved. No part of this work may be reproduced or utilised in any form or by any means, electronic or mechanical, including photocopying, recording or by any information storage and retrieval system, without the prior written permission of the publisher.

Ella's Kitchen (Brands) Limited asserts the moral right to be identified as the author of this work.

ISBN 9780600635765

A CIP catalogue record for this book is available from the British Library.

Typeset in Cooper Light and Ella's Kitchen

Printed and bound in China

Created by Ella's Kitchen and Harris + Wilson

10 9 8 7 6 5 4 3 2 1

Design and styling: Anita Mangan
Photographer: Jonathan Cherry
Art direction: Sarah Ford
Managing editor: Judy Barratt
Design assistant: Abigail Read
Assistant production manager: Lucy Carter
Production controller: Grace O'Byrne
Food stylist: Vicki Savage & Jayne Cross
Recipe testing: Emma Jane Frost & Nicola Graimes

Disclaimer

A few recipes include nuts and nut derivatives. Anyone with a known nut allergy must avoid these. Children under the age of three with a family history of nut allergy, asthma, eczema or any type of allergy are also advised to avoid eating dishes that contain nuts.

Some recipes contain honey. It is advised not to feed honey to children under 12 months old.

Every care should be taken when cooking with and for children. Neither the author, the contributors nor the publisher can accept any liability for any consequences arising from the use of this book, or the information contained herein.

Publisher's notes

Standard level spoon measures are used in the recipes:
1 tablespoon = one 15 ml spoon
1 teaspoon = one 5 ml spoon

Both metric and imperial measurements are given for the recipes. Use one set of measures only, not a mixture of both.

Ovens should be preheated to the specified temperature. If using a fan-assisted oven, follow the manufacturer's instructions for adjusting the time and temperature.

Medium eggs have been used throughout, unless otherwise specified. Herbs are fresh, unless otherwise specified. Use low-salt stock, and avoid adding salt to recipes altogether.

Certified

B Corporation

We're super proud to be a certified B Corporation

We passionately believe that businesses can and should be a force for good, so that's why we joined the B Corp movement.

B Corps aspire not only to be the best in the world but the best for the world.

As members of B Corp we actively contribute to solving social and environmental problems as well as making sure that we are a super tip-top employer which promotes the wellbeing of our people.

It's what we've always been about, but now we have lots of other friends in the business community who think that way too.

And we're passionate about leading the movement in the UK to encourage other business to become B Corps too, because then the world will be an even better place.

We hope you enjoy this book. Please return or renew it by the due date.You can renew it at **www.norfolk.gov.uk/libraries** or by using our free library app. Otherwise you can phone **0344 800 8020** - please have your library card and PIN ready.You can sign up for email reminders too.

NORFOLK COUNTY COUNCIL
LIBRARY AND INFORMATION SERVICE

NORFOLK ITEM

30129 083 730 151

Ella's kitchen

the Cook Book

100 yummy recipes to inspire big and little cooks

hamlyn

Contents

Foreword by Ella's dad

My wife Alison and I became first-time parents when our daughter Ella was born. The new responsibility, the sense of fulfilment and the unlimited outpouring of love are – I'm sure – felt by virtually every new parent. Parenthood really is life-changing. By the time our son Paddy was born, I'd been an active father for three years – and I loved it.

I experienced first-hand the challenges of weaning and the issues involved with introducing two babies (and then toddlers) to new foods. Ella, like the vast majority of little ones, was selective about what she wanted to try, often with no consistency from one day to the next. My solution was to do what I do best: to be silly and childlike. I thought up food-based games. I tried to encourage her to look at her food, and to touch it, smell it and even listen to it, before finally eating it. I invented stories and made up songs; I created imaginary friends and performed 'magic'. I turned mealtimes into events that were messy, noisy and interactive. Ella laughed and I laughed. Best of all, Ella showed willingness to experiment with and enjoy her food. My efforts worked with Paddy, too.

Then, I had my 'lightbulb' moment: healthy food could be – and should be – fun for young kids. This single notion was to be the inspiration for Ella's Kitchen. I gave up my job and set about creating a range of foods for babies, toddlers and young children. I wanted to develop a brand that would bring together three elements that often work against each other in prepared children's food: healthiness, handiness and fun.

At Ella's we always try to look at life from a child's point of view – with an open mind and with all our senses. My strong belief is that the more a young child is involved with his or her food – whether that's choosing it, preparing it, playing with it or eating it independently – the more likely he or she is to give it a try and to go on to enjoy it. With such a positive start, children are far more likely to grow up to have a healthy attitude not just towards mealtimes, but towards their whole diet and overall wellbeing, too.

We've created this book to build further on the Ella's Kitchen ethos – to help even the youngest of children develop healthy eating habits that will last their lifetime. I hope that it will give you and your family far more than recipes for fantastic children's food. I hope that the shared experience of creating dishes together – from making the shopping list and buying and preparing the ingredients to discovering how they feel and spotting their rainbow of colours – will help to strengthen your bond. The ultimate expression of this bond is when you sit down to eat together with big smiles, enjoying the meal that you have created.

Our Ella's Kitchen family has had great fun experimenting as we've developed the ideas for this book. Now that it has found its way to your family kitchen, I hope that your mealtime experiences are equally good!

Keep smiling

Paul

Paul, Ella's dad x
Follow me on Twitter: @Paul_Lindley

In Ella's own words

Ever since I was very young, I've loved playing and experimenting with food. Some of my favourite memories are centred around foody things. One of my earliest recollections of cooking is from when I was about four and my friends and I created a chocolate café, complete with chocolate cookies, chocolate soup and chocolate milkshake – although I'm pretty sure everything tasted the same!

My favourite school subject is Food Technology – we learn how to cook more independently and how to make more complex dishes. I love coming home from school on Mondays with a freshly made pizza or pasta bake.

All of my family enjoy creating new meals and our oven is never put to rest. One of my favourite sensations is when I wake up on a Sunday morning to the mouth-watering smell of pancakes, or when I get home from school to the appetising aroma of dinner. Whether it's curry or roast, my dad always makes sure that our meals are healthy and yummy at the same time. My brother and I are both very involved with the family's cooking and we often take it in turns to make dinner.

Once, for my grandma's birthday, we each cooked a course. My little brother cooked the appetiser; my dad, a starter; my mum, the main; and I made dessert. It made my grandma's birthday extra amazingly, superbly special! I think that letting kids get involved with food from a young age and letting them try new, exciting things is very important. I hope you have loads of fun with our cook book!

Ella x

Our cook book

A bit about using this book

We hope that this book is far more than just a cook book. It's about encouraging your children to embark upon a lifetime's adventure with food. As you involve them in every step of the cooking process, you'll help them to develop food confidence. Their curiosity will turn them into excited culinary explorers – they'll want to smell, touch and taste the ingredients, and they'll love how foods transform during cooking. By taking time to follow a recipe together, you are sharing quality time during which you laugh together, enjoy each other's company *and* make something yummy.

From the beginning

If you're a first-time parent embarking upon weaning, take a look at our simple weaning guide on pages 10–11. Our tips provide the essence of how to introduce an exciting array of foods to your baby from their first mouthfuls. If you have a toddler and a baby and want to make meals that will accommodate both, look out for the 'easy to mash' icon (see opposite), which flags up the recipes that are also great to mash for your tiny family members.

Getting stuck in

Tots and toddlers make wonderful helpers, and at Ella's we believe that messiness is all part of the fun: there's lots to stir, mix, squish, pour, squeeze and decorate. We love it when little fingers are prepared to feel the textures of different foods during the cooking process and then make foods look beautiful on the plate – even if that's just arranging fruit slices in a pattern.

Lots of the recipes have suggestions for how little ones can help; and be sure to dip into our inspirational activity pages, which are intended to create general excitement about the world of food.

At the end of the book there are some handy stickers. You can use them as rewards for your children for super helping or fabulous eating, and as markers for their favourite recipes, too.

Saving time

We know you're busy, so it's been really important to us that we provide recipes that are suitable for your lifestyle. They've all come from parents like you and have been road-tested by Ella's Kitchen families and friends.

Wherever we can, we've included handy hints and shortcuts. For example, we've suggested when you could use an Ella's Kitchen pouch as a shortcut for a sauce. Also, we've included a chapter called 'Hooray for the Weekend', which you can dip into when you have more time to cook as a family.

Sensible shopping lists

All the recipes in the book use healthy ingredients. Our team of nutritionists has selected and approved every one to ensure that you can provide your children with a nourishing diet. We use less sugar and fewer sugary ingredients, and avoid using salt whenever possible. Instead, we season with a range of herbs and spices. Whenever you can, use low-salt or no-salt versions of stock cubes and other ingredients that might already have salt in them.

We recommend that you use organic foods, especially for the fresh ingredients. We believe that organic farmers produce their foods using the purest farming standards.

We've tried to ensure that the recipes call for ingredients that you can find easily. All should be available in your local supermarket, and you may even already have lots of them in your cupboards.

We believe that to have a truly healthy relationship with food, children should never feel guilty or awkward about anything they eat. Healthy puddings – and treats for special occasions – are fine, and all our sweet recipes minimise the use of refined sugar.

Freezer friendly

Your freezer is your friend when feeding a family. Use it well and on busy days it will keep you fed with almost zero effort. Look for the freezer icon (see below) on recipes in this book that can be frozen.

Freeze food in a freezer set at -18°C (0°F). Meat dishes will freeze safely for up to four weeks; vegetarian dishes (including fruit pies), cakes and biscuits can freeze for up to three months. Always label your foods with the date of freezing. When defrosting, always do so covered in the fridge, or in an airtight container submersed in cold water, or in a microwave. Eat, cook or reheat foods (as appropriate) as soon as they are defrosted. When reheating, always do so until piping hot all the way through. Do not refreeze.

Key to icons

At the top of every recipe you'll find a combination of the following icons to help make cooking for, and with, your little ones as easy as it can be.

First foods for tiny taste buds

1 When to wean

All babies are different – some may be ready for solid foods earlier than others, and some will take to weaning more quickly. Department of Health recommendations are to start weaning around the age of 6 months but never before 17 weeks.

Look for signs that your baby is ready to wean. They should be able to sit up and hold their head steady, and put an object, like a spoon, into their mouth accurately. Even then, if they push food back out with their tongue, wait a week and try again.

Check with your health visitor if you are offering your baby food before they turn 6 months of age (but after 17 weeks).

2 Ready, steady, go!

Little by little

When you begin weaning, offer food at a time when your little one is not too tired or hungry – in the middle of, or just after, a daytime milk feed is a good idea.

Baby knows best

Most babies know when they've had enough to eat. If your little one doesn't seem to want any more, don't force the issue. You'll know they have had enough when they clamp their mouth shut, push away the bowl or spoon, or turn their head away.

Smoothly does it

Smooth purées give the best texture for tiny tummies. Veggies and hard fruits (such as apples) will need to be peeled, chopped, then steamed or boiled until soft before you blend them; soft fruits (such as bananas) can be blended straight away.

Model parent

Try to eat with your little one as much as you can so they can learn to copy you. Show them how yummy you think veggies are!

3 Veg it, switch it, repeat it

Babies have 30,000 taste buds in their tiny mouths – that's three times more than grown-ups – so new food is big news.

One by one

Introducing single veg tastes followed by pure veg blends early on in weaning gets tiny tastebuds used to savoury flavours. Get your little ones loving a variety of tastes with a rainbow of veggies. It can take up to eight tries for your little one to enjoy a new food. So keep trying!

First weeks of weaning

Here is a handy little planner for the first few weeks of weaning. But remember, this is just a guide: follow your baby's lead and be led by his or her appetite.

Week 1: Once a day

Try 1–2 spoonfuls of purée just after your baby's lunchtime milk (or whenever suits you and your baby best).

Week 2: Once or twice a day

Your baby can now slurp up to about 5 spoonfuls of purée at each meal.

Week 3: Twice a day

Offer up to 10 spoonfuls at each meal – a feast!

Week 4: Two or three times a day

10 or more spoonfuls will tingle tiny taste buds at breakfast, lunch and dinner – let your baby tell you when he or she has had enough.

What to give your baby

If you do start weaning before your baby turns 6 months, start by offering a variety of pure veg, and then begin to introduce fruit and gluten-free cereals after a couple of weeks.

Once your baby is 6 months old and ready to wean, he or she can begin to enjoy puréed vegetables and fruit and cereals. From 6 months of age, little ones can eat foods that contain allergens, such as cereals containing gluten (e.g. wheat or oats), yogurt, cheese, fish or soya. Chat with your health visitor if you have allergies in the family. When you are ready, you can also offer protein foods, such as meat and pulses, as these provide an important source of iron for little ones.

Broccoli   Carrot   Peas

Parsnip   Green beans   Cauliflower

Meat   Fish   Yogurt

Wheat   Cheese

Keep up the milk

As the first steps in weaning are just about taste, it's really important that babies keep to their usual routine and amounts when it comes to milk feeds – they still need all the goodness in breast milk or formula to keep them healthy.

Remember, all little ones are different and may take to weaning differently – always be led by your baby's appetite.

From mush to mash + beyond

All babies are different. They may reach the following stages a bit earlier or later than we've suggested here, but that's totally normal. Remember that lots of the recipes in this book can be mashed up or blended for babies at 7 months onwards, too.

Look for the 'easy to mash' icon

4–5 months

Chat to your health visitor if you think your little one might be ready to wean before the age of 6 months (but after 17 weeks).

How do I eat?

I can swallow smooth, puréed food with the texture of pouring cream.

What can I eat?

Tiny tastes of a variety of smoothly puréed vegetables, followed by fruit and gluten-free cereals. Just a few spoonfuls a day.

6–7 months

How do I eat?

Using my tongue, I can move thicker purées from side to side in my mouth.

What can I eat?

A variety of vegetables and fruits. I can now eat thicker purées and can try soft finger foods, such as cooked vegetable sticks about the size of an adult's index finger. Introduce allergen foods one by one, such as cereals containing gluten, yogurt, soya, fish and eggs. Introduce protein foods, such as pulses and meat.

7–9 months

How do I eat?

I can mush up soft lumps with my tongue and I am getting better at grasping finger foods and putting them in my mouth. Let me hold a spoon and I'll try scooping.

What can I eat?

Fork-mashed fruit and veg, softly cooked minced beef and turkey, and mashed-down lentils and beans. I can eat a wider range of finger foods, such as bread or toast soldiers, scrambled egg and large pasta pieces.

10–12 months

How do I eat?

I may now have a tooth or two, so I love to munch on larger chunks. I can eat finger foods with a bit of bite and I can pick up smaller pieces of food with my pincer grip.

What can I eat?

Whole peas, beans and sweetcorn, firmer cooked veg and larger pieces of softly cooked meat, as well as raw vegetable sticks, such as cucumber or avocado.

Tiny tums and energy needs

Babies need lots of calories and nutrients to fuel their super-fast growth. In fact, per kilo of their body weight, they need more calories than you do.

However, your baby's tummy is still tiny and it can't hold a lot of food in one go. From around 10 months, it's important to give your little one three meals and two nutritious snacks each day, as well as at least 500 ml/17 fl oz of his or her usual milk.

> I use up loads of energy because I'm growing fast and learning to roll, crawl, pull myself up and even take my first tiny steps.

Handy healthy snacks

Try your baby on the following healthy snacks from around 7–9 months old, depending upon when your baby is ready.

- ☺ Pitta slices with hummus or cream cheese
- ☺ Breadsticks and dips
- ☺ Cubes of cheese
- ☺ Cooked broccoli 'trees' and carrot sticks
- ☺ Cooked pasta shapes – try the spinach and tomato varieties to provide some interesting colours

Once your baby turns 10–12 months old, blueberries, raspberries and strawberries make good snacks, too.

13

Learning about food

Research shows that little ones might be more willing to try new foods if they've explored them with all their amazing senses first. So let them get stuck in! Then, as they get older, you can teach them in the simplest terms how all that delicious goodness is helping them to grow up strong and healthy.

Good in every sense

Even in the first stages of weaning, babies can learn to appreciate the sights, smells and textures of food. As your little one learns to express himself or herself using face-pulling, sounds and eventually words, he or she will find many ways to tell you what they think. Even if at the start you're doing all the talking, your baby is taking it all in and will respond with delighted coos, squeals – and grimaces!

Play a game of squeezing eyes tight as you present foods with different smells. Older children will be able to describe or even identify them.

Looks lovely

Lots of different colours and shapes on the plate look more appetising for little ones. Each time your baby reaches for a food, talk about the colour and, when foods are whole, the shapes.

Sounds scrummy

What makes an onion sizzle in a pan? Why does a carrot stick crunch? How is that different from the crunch of an apple? What's the sound of a smoothie slurp? When we like something, we say 'Mmmmm'. Encourage your little one to listen to foody sounds as you cook, eat and enjoy their meals together.

Tastes terrific

There's no reason why exploring tastes can't become child's play. Throughout weaning, you can introduce some really zingy flavours. Sit at the table and play a tasting game. Try little pieces of pineapple, or strips of red, green and yellow pepper – any distinctive flavours work really well. Poke out a tongue and give foods an exploratory lick.

Smells super

Our sense of smell is closely linked to our sense of taste. Encourage your baby to smell his or her food before eating it. Lead the way: waft it under your own nose and make happy, yummy sounds before you offer it to your baby, who will soon learn to take a sniff and copy what you do.

Feels fab

Allow your baby to pick up his or her food to feel how bumpy, rough or smooth it is. Again, you do the describing. Remember that babies do a lot of 'feeling' with their tongues as well as with their fingers.

Eat a rainbow

Exploring different colours in food is not just about creating excitement – eating fruit and vegtables in all the colours of the rainbow will give your baby a wide range of vitamins and minerals to help their body grow and develop.

Here's our rainbow of favourite foods:

Red: Cherry, cranberry, pepper, radish, raspberry, red onion, strawberry, tomato

Orange: Apricot, butternut squash, carrot, mango, orange, papaya, peach, pepper, pumpkin, sweet potato

Yellow: Banana, lemon, parsnip, pineapple, starfruit

Green: Apple, artichoke, asparagus, broccoli, cabbage, courgette, grape, kiwi, lime, pear, spinach

Blue: Blueberry

Purple: Beetroot, blackberry, blackcurrant, grape, plum

Colour a rainbow! Which colours of fruit and veg has your little one eaten this week? Make a picture using those colours.

The wheel of scrummy goodness

It's good to introduce children to the idea that food helps us grow and gives us energy. Use this wheel as a starting point to teach your toddler about the nutrients that help keep him or her healthy.

Vitamin A to help you see

Vitamin C for healthy gums

Iron for a healthy brain

B-vitamins for bouncy energy

Calcium for strong bones

Zinc for immunity

Yummy lunches
+
speedy snacks

Have fantastically fruity fun with my veeeery streeeetchy cheese on toast.

Love, Ella x

slurp!

squelch!

Brilliant butternut squash soup

serves 4 + 4 adults + kids | prep 15 minutes | cook 30–40 minutes

This soup hits the spot for a family welly walk – these children loved it. Perhaps it's the soup's sweet, rich flavour that got their senses going – or its *reeeally* bright orange colour. Add the cardamom if your little one is up for trying new flavours.

What you need

About 1.4 kg/3 lb 2 oz **butternut squash**, cut into 2.5 cm/1 in dice

Olive oil, for roasting

8 **sage** leaves, finely chopped

50 g/1¾ oz **unsalted butter**

1 **onion**, chopped

Seeds from 5 **cardamom pods**, crushed (optional)

1 litre/1¾ pints reduced-salt **vegetable stock**

Crème fraîche, to serve

What to do

1. Preheat the oven to 200°C/400°F/Gas Mark 6.

2. Put the squash cubes in a roasting tray, sprinkle with a little olive oil and scatter over the chopped sage. Toss the cubes so that they are well coated in the oil, then roast them in the oven for 15–20 minutes or until the cubes are soft and turning golden. Remove the squash from the oven and set aside.

3. Melt the butter in a large saucepan over a medium heat, then add the onion and fry until soft. Add the crushed cardamom pods (if using) and the vegetable stock. Then add the squash. Give it all a stir and bring to a boil. Reduce the heat and simmer for 15–20 minutes, until all the ingredients are soft and pulpy and the liquid has reduced a little. Remove the pan from the heat and use a hand blender to whiz the mixture until smooth.

4. Serve the soup with a small dollop of crème fraîche.

❄ If you are freezing this dish, do so before adding the crème fraîche.

Squashy tasks

Can I help?

Digging out the squash seeds with a spoon is a great way to get children involved in the early stages of the soup, as well as sprinkling over the sage before roasting. Ask your little one to watch as you blend the soup – can they see how it changes before their very eyes? Take care that the hot liquid doesn't splash, though.

Slurpy chicken noodle bowl

serves **2+2** adults + kids · prep **10** minutes · cook **5** minutes

Easy to make, this miso noodle soup is a great way to use up leftover roast meat. We've used leftover roast chicken, but roast pork or beef would be equally tasty, or even cooked firm fish fillets or prawns. Have all the ingredients ready before you start, as it's quick to cook.

What you need

5 cm/2 inch piece fresh **ginger**, peeled and sliced into thick rounds

200 g/7 oz no-salt medium **wholewheat** or **egg noodles**

150 g/5½ oz small **broccoli florets**

2 handfuls **sugar snap peas**, or 50 g/1¾ oz **kale**, finely chopped

3 **spring onions**, thinly sliced diagonally

1 small **red pepper,** deseeded and thinly sliced

250 g/9 oz **cooked chicken breast**, shredded or chopped

2–3 tablespoons dark **miso paste**, to taste

1 teaspoon **sesame oil**

1 teaspoon toasted **sesame seeds**, for sprinkling (optional)

What to do

1. Pour 1 litre/1¾ pints water into a large saucepan, add the ginger and bring to the boil. Stir in the noodles and cook for 2 minutes, then add the broccoli and cook for another 2 minutes.

2. Add the sugar snap peas or kale, 2 of the spring onions and the red pepper and cook for another minute, until the noodles are cooked and the vegetables remain slightly crunchy.

3. Strain the cooking water into a jug and reserve, discarding the ginger.

4. Divide the noodles and vegetables between 4 serving bowls and add the cooked chicken.

5. Measure out 700ml/1¼ pints of the cooking water and pour away any surplus. Stir the miso paste and sesame oil into the cooking water until combined, then pour it into the serving bowls. Sprinkle over the remaining spring onion and the sesame seeds, if using, then serve.

I can't slurp

Colour me in

I can!

Veggie-tastic samosas

Easy for tiny hands to grasp and bursting with good stuff, our veggie samosas are a perfect snack served at home, on the go, or in a lunchbox. Use our handy folding guide to make beautiful little parcels.

What you need

2 teaspoons **vegetable oil**, plus extra for oiling and brushing

100 g/3½ oz peeled and deseeded **butternut squash**, diced

50 g/1¾ oz **carrot** (about 1), diced

50 g/1¾ oz **cauliflower floret**, grated

4 tablespoons frozen **peas**

1 tablespoon **lemon juice**

1 teaspoon **garam masala**

8 sheets of **filo pastry**

Nigella seeds, for sprinkling

What to do

1. Preheat the oven to 180°C/350°F/Gas Mark 4. Lightly oil 2 baking trays.

2. Heat the oil in a large frying pan over a medium heat, add the vegetables and cook for 7 minutes until slightly softened. Stir in the lemon juice and garam masala.

3. Brush 1 sheet of filo with a little oil and place a second sheet on top. Cut the sandwiched sheets into 3 strips lengthways.

4. Place 1 heaped tablespoon of the vegetable filling near the bottom corner of each strip of pastry. Fold the strips as shown in the diagram below to make 3 samosas, then brush the far edge with oil and fold it over to seal. Brush the tops with oil, place on a baking tray and sprinkle with nigella seeds. Repeat with the rest of the filo and filling to make 12 samosas.

5. Bake the samosas for 15–20 minutes until light golden and crisp. Serve warm or cold.

Handy samosa folding guide

Cut the filo pastry into 3 equally sized strips. Put a blob of filling in the bottom corner of each one and fold over and over...

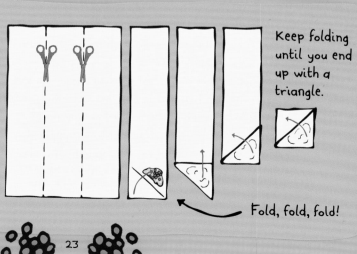

Keep folding until you end up with a triangle.

Fold, fold, fold!

Very nice dips for crunchy veg sticks

Fed up with dipping into hummus or mayo? You'll get your little ones happily munching and crunching vegetable sticks all day with these tasty, adventurous dips that are full of complementary flavours and textures. Carrot, celery, cucumber and pepper make the perfect dipping sticks.

Aubergine, pine nut + tomato dip

serves **4** | prep **5** minutes | cook **45** minutes

1 large **aubergine**

25 g/1 oz **pine nuts**

2 tablespoons **sun-dried tomato purée**

1. Preheat the oven to 200°C/400°F/Gas Mark 6.

2. Prick the aubergine all over with a fork and place it in the oven; bake it for 45 minutes until soft. Allow to cool.

3. In a small frying pan, dry-fry the pine nuts until golden.

4. Scoop the aubergine flesh from the skin and place it in a bowl with the pine nuts and tomato purée. Blend to a coarse paste with a hand blender.

Roast pepper, cream cheese + basil dip

serves **4** | prep **5** minutes | cook **30** minutes

2 **red peppers**

1 teaspoon **olive oil**

200 g/7 oz **cream cheese**

8 **basil** leaves, finely chopped

1. Preheat the oven to 200°C/400°F/Gas Mark 6.

2. Rub the peppers with the oil and place them on a baking sheet. Roast the peppers for 30 minutes until slightly charred, then place them in a large plastic bag and allow to cool. Peel off the skin and remove the seeds.

3. Place the pepper flesh in a food processor with the cream cheese and blend to a coarse paste. Stir in the basil.

Smoked mackerel dip

serves **4** | prep **5** minutes

2 **smoked mackerel** fillets, skin and bones removed

5 tablespoons **low-fat natural yogurt**

1. Place the mackerel and yogurt in a food processor and blend to a coarse paste. Or, if you don't have a processor, use a hand blender, or flake the fish into a bowl and mash it with a fork. Stir through the yogurt.

Crunchy veggie
dipping sticks

Roast pepper, cream
cheese + basil dip

Aubergine, pine nut
+ tomato dip

Smoked mackerel dip

Bubble + squeak patties

Serves 8 · prep 5 minutes · cook 12 minutes

Somehow even the greenest greens taste great in bubble and squeak, and these little veggie fritters are a brilliant way to use up some leftover veg.

What you need

2–3 tablespoons **olive oil**

½ **onion** (or a couple of spring onions), finely chopped

450 g/1 lb **potatoes**, cooked and mashed

225 g/8 oz cooked **Brussels sprouts** (or broccoli or cabbage), chopped

½ teaspoon **dried mixed herbs** (or some finely chopped parsley)

2 **eggs**, beaten

Freshly ground **black pepper**, to taste

Listen up!

Bubble and squeak is so called because the potato and vegetables make popping and squeaking sounds as they cook in the pan. Ask your little one to listen out for them.

What to do

1. Heat 1 tablespoon of the oil in a frying pan and fry the onion over a low heat for 3–4 minutes until soft.

2. Put the mashed potato and sprouts in a bowl and stir together. Add the cooked onion, herbs and eggs, season with black pepper, and mix well.

3. Put a further 1 tablespoon of the oil in the frying pan and warm over a medium heat.

4. Fry spoonfuls of the mixture for about 6–8 minutes, turning once using a fish slice, until lightly browned on both sides. (You may need to cook the mixture in batches – using some more oil, if necessary – depending upon the size of your pan.)

5. Serve immediately with a handful of grilled cherry tomatoes and any leftover cold meat you have to hand.

 These patties can be frozen before or after they are cooked.

Tasty Thai rice

This quick and easy one-pan meal can be easily adapted to suit family preferences, or jazzed up with more adult flavours at the end of cooking…so one dish fits all.

What you need

1 tablespoon **coconut oil** or other flavourless **vegetable oil**

1 **onion**, finely chopped

2 **garlic** cloves, finely chopped

100 g/3½ oz **cauliflower** florets, grated

1 **red pepper**, deseeded and diced

2.5 cm/1 inch piece **fresh ginger**, peeled and grated

2 **lemon grass** sticks, outer layer removed, inside finely chopped

1 **kaffir lime** leaf, finely sliced (optional)

100 g/3½ oz frozen **peas**

350 g/12 oz cooked, cold **wholegrain**, **jasmine** or **basmati rice** (about 150 g/5½ oz uncooked grains)

2 teaspoons reduced-salt **soy sauce**

2 large **eggs**, lightly beaten

Freshly ground black **pepper**

Steamed **green vegetables**, such as broccoli or kale, to serve (optional)

40 g/1½ oz unsalted roasted **peanuts**, finely chopped, to serve (optional)

sriracha chilli sauce, to serve (optional)

What to do

1. Heat a large wok over a high heat. Add the oil, followed by the onion, garlic, cauliflower, pepper and ginger and stir-fry for 5 minutes.

2. Reduce the heat to medium, add the lemon grass, kaffir lime leaf, if using, and peas and stir-fry for 2 minutes until the peas are tender.

3. Add the cold, cooked rice and stir-fry until heated through and piping hot, about 2 minutes.

4. Stir in the soy sauce and season with black pepper. Make a large hole in the middle, tip in the eggs and let them cook a little, stirring as you would with scrambled eggs. When the eggs start to firm up, start to fold them into the rice until you have flecks of egg throughout.

5. Serve the rice in bowls topped with your choice of green vegetables, peanuts and sriracha (for the grown-ups).

Cooked rice

The cooked rice needs to be completely cold before you start to stir-fry. To do this, simply cook the rice according to the packet instructions and then either spread it out on a baking tray or put it into a large bowl and turn occasionally to separate the grains to cool it quickly. Once the rice has cooled to room temperature (ideally within an hour of cooking), it can be used in the stir-fry. If you aren't using the rice straightaway, store the cooled rice in the refrigerator for up to 2 days.

Quickly does it quiche

Perfect for a family lunch or a picnic, this easy-peasy quiche is quick to make and great for little hands to hold while munching. You could make it ahead and freeze it in bite-sized portions, which makes it handy for a lunch or snack on the run.

What you need

350 g/12 oz ready-made **shortcrust pastry**

Flour, for dusting

1 tablespoon **sunflower oil**

1 large **onion**, sliced

250 g/9 oz **unsmoked back bacon**, roughly chopped

3 **eggs**, beaten

2 tablespoons finely chopped **parsley** (or thyme)

100 ml/3½ fl oz **whole milk**

50 g/1¾ oz **Cheddar cheese**, grated

Go veggie

For a vegetarian option, fry the onion with 200 g/7 oz carrot and 200 g/7 oz diced aubergine for 5 minutes. Allow to cool, then arrange in the base of the pastry case. Pour over the milk and egg mixture, scatter with the Cheddar, then cook as in the meat version.

What to do

1. Preheat the oven to 200°C/400°F/Gas Mark 6.

2. Roll out the pastry on a floured surface and use it to line a 22 cm/8½ inch round quiche tin. Place a piece of scrunched-up baking parchment inside the pastry case and fill it with some baking beans (or dried lentils if you can't get hold of baking beans).

3. Place the tin on a baking sheet and bake blind for 10 minutes until the pastry is just starting to colour. Remove the baking beans and parchment and return the pastry to the oven for a further 5 minutes until golden.

4. Meanwhile, heat the oil in a large frying pan and fry the onion and bacon together for 5 minutes until cooked. In a bowl or large measuring jug, mix together the eggs, herbs and milk.

5. Scatter the bacon and onion mixture evenly into the baked pastry case and pour in the milk and egg mixture. Scatter over the Cheddar. Bake in the oven for 25–30 minutes until golden.

choo choo

31

Clever tomato sauce

serves 4 · **prep** 15 minutes · **cook** 12 minutes

This sauce is clever for two reasons: first, we can think of lots of ways to use it –
see opposite for five of them – and, second, it's packed to the brim with veggie goodness.

What you need

1 **carrot**, diced

200 g/7 oz **butternut squash**, diced

50 g/1¾ oz **frozen peas**, defrosted

415 g/14¾ oz can reduced-sugar and salt **baked beans**

400 g/14 oz can **chopped tomatoes**

200 g/7 oz **tomatoes**, chopped

What to do

1. In a saucepan of boiling water, boil the carrot, squash and peas for 7–8 minutes until tender, then drain and return to the pan. Keeping the pan off the heat, add the baked beans and purée the mixture with a hand blender until smooth.

2. Return the pan to the heat. Add both the canned and fresh tomatoes and bring everything to the boil. Reduce the heat and simmer for 4–5 minutes until the fresh tomatoes are soft and pulpy. Remove the pan from the heat and purée again until you have a beautifully smooth sauce.

colour me in

32

Grow your own

Turn your windowsill into a microleaf garden with edible plants that are quick to grow and scrummy to eat. What better way to learn where food comes from?

(1)

Find your flavours

Rocket, cress, basil and pea shoots all make brilliant microplants – you can harvest their baby leaves within two weeks. Choose some greens you'll use – rocket for pizza, basil for pasta sauce, cress for sandwiches. Yum!

② Paint a pot

Little brown pots are the perfect canvas for tiny tot decorations. Find some stickers and paints and get creative. Spots, stripes or splodges – anything goes.

③ Plant the seeds

Fill the pots with damp soil and scatter in some seeds. Sprinkle over a little more soil and place your pots on a sunny windowsill.

Turn your pot into a face with googly eyes and sticker-lips, then grow some cress in it. Soon enough your face has grown green hair!

Tea-set milk jugs make perfect mini-watering cans for tiny fingers and tiny plants.

④ Harvest the leaves

Remember to talk about the leaves – their colour, shape and smell – as you pick. Use them straight away.

Fantastically fruity cheese on toast

makes 1 · prep 5 minutes · cook 4–6 minutes

This is a new dimension in cheese on toast that needs both hands to eat it. Teaming creamy mozzarella with juicy blueberries is just genius. Serve it as a snack at any time of the day.

What you need

Unsalted butter, for spreading

2 thick slices **farmhouse white bread**

1 slice **ham**

40 g/1½ oz **mozzarella cheese**, drained and sliced

20 g/¾ oz **blueberries**, lightly crushed with the back of a fork

What to do

1. Lightly butter 1 side of each slice of bread. Turn 1 slice unbuttered side up and top with the ham, mozzarella and blueberries. Sandwich with the remaining slice of bread, butter side up.

2. Heat a small frying pan and dry-fry the sandwich for 2–3 minutes on each side until the bread is golden and the mozzarella has melted. Serve immediately.

To mix it up, why not try different combinations of ingredients? Follow the steps above, replacing the ham, mozzarella and blueberries with either of the fillings below.

Tuna + spring onion melt

Unsalted **butter**, for spreading

2 thick slices **farmhouse granary bread**

2 teaspoons **tomato purée**

40 g/1½ oz canned **tuna**, or **sardines in tomato sauce**, drained and mashed

1 small **spring onion**, finely chopped

40 g/1½ oz **mozzarella cheese**, drained and sliced

Italian flag toastie

Unsalted **butter**, for spreading

2 thick slices **farmhouse wholemeal bread**

2 teaspoons **red pesto** (see page 97)

½ small ripe **avocado**, mashed

40 g/1½ oz **mozzarella cheese**, drained and sliced

A few basil leaves

Mighty grain & herby salad

serves 4–6 | prep 15 minutes | cook 15 minutes

Serve this crunchy salad as a side dish, or make a meal of it by topping with crumbled cheese, a boiled or poached egg, or slices of ham, cooked chicken or salmon.

What you need

60 g/2¼ oz multi-coloured **quinoa**, rinsed

1 red eating **apple**

7 cm/2¾ inch piece of **cucumber**

40 g/1½ oz **broccoli** florets, finely chopped, stalk and all

3 tablespoons finely chopped **mint leaves**

2 tablespoons finely chopped **flat-leaf parsley**

25 g/1 oz unsalted shelled **pistachio nuts,** loose skins rubbed off, finely chopped (optional)

For the dressing

Juice of 1 small **lemon**

2 tablespoons **extra virgin olive oil**

½ teaspoon **Dijon mustard**

1 teaspoon runny **honey**

What to do

1. To cook the quinoa, place it in a small saucepan and pour in enough cold water to cover by 2 cm/¾ inch. Bring to the boil, then reduce the heat and simmer, part-covered, for 15 minutes or until tender. Drain well and leave to cool for 10 minutes.

2. Meanwhile, core the apple, cut it into small bite-sized pieces, place in a serving bowl and squeeze over some of the lemon juice from the dressing ingredients. Turn the apple in the lemon juice to prevent it turning brown.

3. Halve the piece of cucumber lengthways and, using a teaspoon, scoop out and discard the seeds. Chop the rest into small bite-sized pieces and add to the apple in the bowl with the broccoli, herbs and cooled quinoa. Turn until mixed together.

4. In a small bowl or a cup, whisk together the dressing ingredients and pour over the salad, then gently turn it all around to coat. Scatter over the pistachios, if using, and serve the salad at room temperature.

Mix 'n' match

You can include everyone's favourite fruit and veggies in this flexible recipe. Instead of apple, broccoli and pistachios try equal amounts of pear, grated cauliflower and walnuts; or small chunks of Cheddar cheese, finely chopped spinach and raisins; or chopped pineapple or mango, finely chopped kale and almonds.

Seeds be gone!

Can I help?

Even quite small hands will love being put in charge of a teaspoon and given the job of excavating a cucumber half. Squidgy fun!

39

Tuck-in tortilla toasties

serves **2** · prep **15** minutes · cook **18** minutes

Wrapping up lots of good stuff in a tortilla and then toasting it in a frying pan is a great way to use up leftovers and easy for little ones to hold in their hands to eat. Try out different fillings to get their taste buds tingling.

What you need

2 teaspoons **olive oil**, plus extra for brushing

6 **mushrooms**, thinly sliced

1 **spring onion**, finely chopped

1 small **garlic clove**, finely chopped

2 **flour tortillas**

1 small ripe **avocado**, mashed

50 g/1¾ oz **ham**, finely chopped

75 g/2½ oz **Cheddar cheese**, grated

What to do

1. Heat the oil in a large frying pan over a medium heat and fry the mushrooms for 5 minutes until softened. Add the spring onion and garlic and cook for another minute. Tip the mushroom mixture into a bowl and wipe the pan clean.

2. Lightly brush the frying pan with a little more oil. Lay a tortilla flat in the pan and arrange half of the mushroom mixture over half of it, keeping a clear 3 cm/1¼ inch border around the edge. Now add half of the avocado, ham and cheese on top of the mushrooms. Fold the empty half of the tortilla over the top and press the edges down.

3. Heat the tortilla over a medium heat for 2–3 minutes, then turn it and cook for another 2–3 minutes, until golden.

4. Slide the tortilla onto a chopping board, then prepare the remaining tortilla in the same way. Leave to cool for a couple of minutes, then cut each tortilla into 3 wedges.

Pick me up!

Easy cheesy courgette frittata

Getting grated courgettes into these frittatas is a simple way to sneak some good-for-you greens into a meal. The frittata is delicious warm or cold and makes a great finger food.

What you need

6 **eggs**

250 g/9 oz **Cheddar cheese**, grated

250 g/9 oz **courgette**, coarsely grated

50 g/1¾ oz **pitted black olives**, roughly chopped (optional)

3 **spring onions** or 75 g/2½ oz **leek** or **white onion**, finely chopped

Small pinch of **chilli powder** or **cayenne pepper**

1 tablespoon **olive oil**

What to do

1. Preheat the grill to medium. Crack the eggs into a large bowl and beat well using a balloon whisk. Add the Cheddar, courgette and olives (if using), the spring onions, leeks or white onion, and the chilli powder or cayenne pepper and beat again to combine.

2. Heat the oil in a 30 cm/12 inch frying pan, then pour in the egg mixture and cook over a gentle heat for 2–3 minutes until the base of the frittata is set. Place the frittata under the grill and cook for a further 3–4 minutes until the top is set and golden.

3. Slide the frittata onto a plate and cut into 8 wedges. Serve warm or cold with salad.

Go crackers!

Little ones can have a go at cracking the eggs into the bowl and then take a turn at beating them with a fork or balloon whisk. Who has the fastest action?

Can I help?

More veg

For extra veggie goodness, try adding 75 g/2½ oz of drained no-salt and no-sugar sweetcorn and/or a small, grated carrot to the bowl with the other ingredients in step 1.

Five ways with pitta, wrap or roll fillings

Bored with the same old sandwich fillings? These flavour and texture combinations put the brilliant back into bread – they are delicious, nutritious and, best of all, exciting.

Chompy cheese, carrot + apple

serves 2 | prep 5 minutes

1 tablespoon unsweetened **apple sauce** or **apple purée**

75 g/2½ oz **cream cheese**

1 tablespoon **whole milk**

1 small **carrot**, grated

50 g/1¾ oz **Cheddar cheese**, grated

¼ eating **apple**, grated

2 **pitta breads**, toasted

If you're making your own apple purée, peel, core and chop 1 eating apple. Steam it until soft, then mash with a fork.

Blend the cream cheese with the milk, then fold in 1 tablespoon of the apple sauce or purée. Stir in the carrot, Cheddar and eating apple. Make a slit in the pittas and fill them with the cheese mixture. Cut each pitta in half to serve.

Fit-for-a-king coronation chicken with mango

serves 2 | prep 5 minutes

2 tablespoons **mayonnaise**

2 tablespoons well-chopped **mango**

¼ teaspoon **medium curry powder**

150 g/5½ oz **cooked chicken breast**, torn into small pieces

50 g/1¾ oz **sultanas**

2 **flour tortillas**

2 small handfuls of **rocket**

Put the mayonnaise, mango and curry powder into a bowl and use a hand blender to combine them. Stir in the chicken and sultanas.

Spoon half the mixture in a line across the centre of 1 tortilla, then scatter over half the rocket and roll up tightly. Repeat for the other tortilla.

Cut each tortilla in half to serve.

Crumbly feta + red grape

serves 2 · prep 5 minutes

50 g/1¾ oz **feta cheese**, crumbled

25 g/1 oz finely **chopped walnuts**

1 **celery stick**, finely chopped

50 g/1¾ oz **seedless red grapes**, halved or quartered

2 tablespoons **mayonnaise**

2 **pitta breads**, toasted

Fold all the filling ingredients together in a bowl until well combined.

Make a slit in the pittas and fill with the cheese mixture. Cut each pitta in half to serve.

Sunshine hummus with basil

serves 2 · prep 5 minutes

1 **clementine**, segmented and chopped

100 g/3½ oz **hummus**

1 small **carrot**, grated

1 tablespoon shredded **basil** leaves

2 **flour tortillas**

Mix all the filling ingredients together in a bowl until well combined.

Spoon half the mixture in a line across the centre of 1 tortilla and roll the tortilla up tightly. Repeat for the other tortilla.

Cut each tortilla in half to serve.

Terrific tuna tzatziki with green grapes

serves 2 · prep 5 minutes

200 g/7 oz can **tuna steak** in spring water, drained well

4 tablespoons **tzatziki**

50 g/1¾ oz **seedless green grapes**, halved or quartered

2 **wholemeal rolls**, halved

Mix all the filling ingredients together in a bowl until well combined.

Pile half the filling into each roll. Cut in half to serve.

Nibbly nacho feast

Children will love to dig into this crunchy, gooey feast of flavour – all you need is fingers.

What you need

3 **soft tortillas**

Olive oil, for brushing

3 pinches of smoked paprika

75 g/2½ oz **mozzarella** cheese, grated

Lime wedges, to serve (optional)

For the tomato salsa

3 **tomatoes**, chopped

3 **spring onions**, finely sliced

Juice of ½ **lime** (reserve the other ½ for wedges

A handful of **coriander**, roughly chopped

½ teaspoon smoked paprika

For the avocado salsa

1 ripe **avocado**

1 tablespoon **sweet chilli dipping sauce**

What to do

1. Preheat the grill to medium-high. Grill the tortillas for 2 minutes on each side until light golden and just crisp – they will crisp up further when cooled. Lightly brush the top of each tortilla with oil and sprinkle over a little paprika. Cut them into wedges and leave to cool completely.

2. To make the tomato salsa, mix together the tomatoes, spring onions, lime juice, coriander and smoked paprika. Set aside.

3. To make the avocado salsa, mash the avocado flesh with the chilli sauce. Set aside.

4. Place the tortilla chips on a large heatproof platter, then spoon over the tomato salsa and sprinkle with the cheese. Place under the preheated grill for 2–3 minutes until the cheese has melted.

5. Spoon the avocado salsa over the top and serve with lime wedges.

Colour me in

Dee-licious dinners

How many different
veggies can you
name?
Can you get up to 10?

Love, Ella x

Bouncy bean & pepper pot with garlicky toasts

serves 4–6 · prep 15 minutes · cook 35 minutes · omit garlic toasts

Everyone loves garlic bread and this version is so good dunked into a bowl of hearty Spanish-style vegetarian stew.

What you need

1 large **aubergine**, cut into bite-sized chunks

2 tablespoons **olive oil**, plus extra for drizzling

1 large **onion**, finely chopped

2 large **garlic** cloves, finely chopped

400 g/14 oz can chopped **tomatoes**

200 ml/7 fl oz reduced-salt **vegetable stock**

1 tablespoon **tomato purée**

1 teaspoon **dried oregano**

1–2 teaspoons **smoked paprika**, or to taste

185 g/6½ oz **roasted red peppers** from a jar, drained, rinsed and chopped

400 g/14 oz can **beans**, such as cannellini, haricot, chickpeas or butter beans, drained and rinsed

Juice of ½ **lemon**

A handful of chopped **parsley**

Freshly ground black **pepper**

For the garlic toasts

4 slices crusty country-style **wholemeal bread**

1 large **garlic** clove, halved

What to do

1. Steam the aubergine for 8 minutes or until tender – doing this first will reduce the amount of oil you need.

2. Meanwhile, heat the oil in a large saucepan over a medium heat. Add the onion and cook, covered, for 10 minutes, until soft but not coloured. Uncover, then stir in the garlic and steamed aubergine and cook for 1 minute. Add the chopped tomatoes, stock, tomato purée, oregano, 1 teaspoon of the smoked paprika, the red peppers and beans. Bring to the boil, then reduce the heat to low and simmer, part-covered, for 25 minutes or until reduced and thickened. Season with pepper, then taste and add more paprika if you like.

3. Just before the stew is ready, make the garlic toasts. Heat a large, ridged griddle pan over a high heat (or preheat the grill). Place the bread in the pan and griddle for 3–4 minutes on each side until toasted. Rub the cut-side of the garlic over 1 side of each slice of toast and drizzle with a little olive oil.

4. Add the lemon juice and parsley to the stew and serve in bowls along with the garlic toasts.

❄ Although the stew can be frozen, the garlic toasts will just go soggy, so make these fresh just before serving.

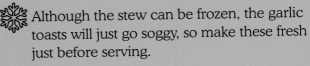

Ella's dad's sweet + sour prawns

serves 4-6 | prep 20 minutes | cook 8 minutes

This recipe from the Lindley family kitchen is a great introduction to the sweet and tangy savoury flavours used in recipes across Asia. We've cut the vegetables into strips, but you can slice them any way you like.

What you need

2 tablespoons **sunflower oil**

250 g/9 oz **raw tiger prawns**, patted dry

4 **spring onions**, thinly sliced

1 **red pepper**, halved, deseeded and thinly sliced

12 **baby sweetcorn**, halved lengthways

2 **carrots**, cut into thin strips

2.5 cm/1 inch piece **fresh ginger**, peeled and finely grated

2 **garlic** cloves, thinly sliced

A large handful of **bean sprouts**

For the sauce

1 tablespoon reduced-salt **light soy sauce**

2 canned **pineapple** rings in natural juice, drained and cut into chunks

2 tablespoons natural **juice from the canned pineapple** (or water)

1 tablespoon **tomato purée**

Juice of 1 **lime**

1 teaspoon **sweet chilli dipping sauce**

1 teaspoon **cornflour**

What to do

1. First make the sauce: put all the ingredients into a bowl and, using a hand blender, blend together until smooth. Set aside.

2. Heat a large wok or frying pan over a medium-high heat, add the oil and the prawns and stir-fry for 3 minutes until the prawns are pink all over. Remove the prawns with a slotted spoon and set aside.

3. Add the spring onions, red pepper, baby sweetcorn and carrots to the wok or pan and stir-fry for 2 minutes. Add the ginger and garlic and cook for another minute until the vegetables are just soft.

4. Add the sauce to the pan with 2 tablespoons water and cook for a further minute until the sauce has thickened. Return the prawns to the pan, add the bean sprouts and heat briefly. Serve immediately with noodles or rice.

❄ If you want to freeze this dish, make sure the prawns you use have not been pre-frozen.

That's magic!

Encourage your little ones to watch the prawns change colour as they cook – as if by magic, their dull grey becomes beautiful pink.

53

Easy peasy veggie risotto

Risotto is so often a winning formula for tiny taste buds. This pea, leek and courgette version is especially easy to put together, but absolutely packed with green-food goodness.

What you need

1 reduced-salt **vegetable stock cube**

200 g/7 oz **easy-cook long grain rice**

75 g/2½ oz **frozen peas**, defrosted

1 tablespoon **olive oil**

1 **leek**, finely chopped

1 **courgette**, finely chopped

150 ml/¼ pint **carrot juice**

Cheddar cheese, grated, to serve

What to do

1. In a large saucepan bring 1 litre/1¾ pints of water to the boil. Crumble in the stock cube and add the rice. Bring the liquid back to the boil, then reduce the heat to low and simmer uncovered for 10–15 minutes until the rice is tender, adding the peas for the last 5 minutes.

2. Drain the rice and pea mixture and set aside.

3. Heat the oil in a large frying pan or wok and cook the leek and courgette for approximately 5 minutes, stirring occasionally, until softened.

4. Add the rice and pea mixture and stir well, then add the carrot juice and continue to cook for a further 2 minutes until piping hot.

5. Serve hot with some grated Cheddar sprinkled on top.

I love my greens!

Magical Moroccan-style chicken

serves 4 | prep 15 minutes | cook 25 minutes

This hotpot-style dish packs in fruit, vegetables and legumes for an all-round nutritional boost. You could purée it and serve it with baby rice for very little ones.

What you need

1 tablespoon **sunflower oil**

2 **chicken breasts** (about 300 g/10½ oz), diced

1 large **carrot**, sliced

1 **leek**, sliced

1 **red pepper**, deseeded and chopped

1 teaspoon **ground cumin**

½ teaspoon **ground cinnamon**

400 g/14 oz can **chickpeas**, drained and rinsed

1 tablespoon **tomato purée**

600 ml/1 pint reduced-salt **vegetable stock**

50 g/1¾ oz **dried apricots**, chopped

A few **coriander leaves**, to serve (optional)

What to do

(1) Heat the oil in a large saucepan and fry the chicken pieces for 4 minutes until golden on all sides. Add the vegetables and spices and fry for a further 2–3 minutes.

(2) Add the chickpeas, tomato purée, vegetable stock and apricots and bring to the boil. Reduce the heat to low, cover and simmer for 15–20 minutes, stirring occasionally, until all the ingredients are tender.

(3) Serve on a bed of couscous sprinkled with the coriander leaves (if using).

Design your own fez

Tasty turkey + rice-packed peppers

Cinnamon and raisins give these stuffed peppers a hint of Middle Eastern flavour. They are a great way to introduce little ones to sweet spices.

What you need

6 **red peppers**

75 g/2½ oz **brown rice**

350 g/12 oz **lean minced turkey**

1 small **onion**, chopped

400 g/14 oz can **chopped tomatoes**

3 tablespoons **tomato purée**

1 tablespoon **Worcestershire sauce**

50 g/1¾ oz **raisins** or **olives**

½ teaspoon **ground cinnamon**

50 g/1¾ oz **mozzarella cheese**, finely chopped

What to do

1. Preheat the oven to 180°C/350°F/Gas Mark 4. Bring a large saucepan of water to the boil (use enough water to cover the peppers). Cut the tops off the peppers and discard them along with the core and seeds. Place the peppers in the boiling water, filling their cavities, and cook for 4 minutes until they begin to soften. Remove the peppers from the water using a slotted spoon (leave the water boiling) and set them aside to drain on kitchen paper, open-end down.

2. Add the rice to the water and cook for 20 minutes until tender.

3. Meanwhile, place the turkey and onion in a large, heavy-based frying pan and cook over a high heat for 8–10 minutes, stirring and breaking up the mince as much as possible. Add the tomatoes, tomato purée, Worcestershire sauce, raisins and cinnamon and stir well. Bring to the boil, then reduce the heat, cover and simmer for 5 minutes.

4. Drain the cooked rice, then stir into the mince mixture. Place the peppers, open-end up, in an ovenproof dish and fill each with some of the mince mixture. Scatter over the mozzarella, then bake in the preheated oven for 15 minutes until the cheese is golden brown.

5 ways

Five ways with green vegetables

Greens don't have to be boring. We've found the perfect partners for green beans, sprouts, broccoli, spinach and courgettes, making the most of all the natural, fresh flavours. High five if your little ones try all five!

Good-for-you green beans

serves 4 | prep 5 minutes | cook 8 minutes

300 g/10½ oz **fine green beans**, trimmed

2 tablespoons **olive oil**

3 **shallots**, finely chopped

50g/1¾ oz **pine nuts**

Cook the beans in boiling water for 5 minutes until just tender, then drain.

Meanwhile, heat the oil in a frying pan and fry the shallots for 2 minutes. Add the pine nuts and fry for 1–2 minutes. Add the cooked beans and stir-fry for 2–3 minutes to heat through. Serve immediately.

Special sprouts

serves 4 | prep 5 minutes | cook 15 minutes

350 g/12 oz **Brussels sprouts**

Unsalted butter, for frying

75 g/2½ oz **unsmoked back bacon**, chopped

1 **garlic** clove, thinly sliced

1 teaspoon **Worcestershire sauce**

Cook the sprouts in boiling water for 10 minutes until just tender, then drain.

Heat the butter in a frying pan and fry the bacon and garlic for 3 minutes until golden. Add the sprouts and fry for 1 minute to heat through, then add the Worcestershire sauce and stir-fry for a few seconds before serving immediately.

Brilliant broccoli

serves 4 · prep 5 minutes · cook 8 minutes

300 g/10½ oz **broccoli florets**

1 tablespoon **toasted sesame oil**

1 tablespoon **sesame seeds**

1 tablespoon reduced-salt **light soy sauce**

Cook the broccoli in boiling water for 4–5 minutes until just tender, then drain.

Heat the oil in a frying pan and toast the sesame seeds for 1 minute until golden. Add the cooked broccoli and the soy sauce and stir-fry, tossing for 1 minute to heat through. Serve immediately.

Splendid spinach

serves 4 · prep 5 minutes · cook 5 minutes

1 kg/2 lb 4 oz packet **frozen spinach**

A pinch of **ground nutmeg**

4 tablespoons **crème fraîche**

1 tablespoon grated **Parmesan cheese**

Cook the spinach in a saucepan according to the packet instructions. Drain and press out as much of the liquid as possible, then return the spinach to the pan.

Add the remaining ingredients and stir to combine. Serve immediately.

Cracking courgettes

serves 4 · prep 5 minutes · cook 7 minutes

1 tablespoon **olive oil**

450 g/1 lb **courgettes**, halved lengthways and sliced

Juice and finely grated zest of ½ **lemon**

A handful of **basil** leaves, finely chopped

Heat the oil in a frying pan and fry the courgettes for 5–6 minutes until golden and just tender.

Remove from the heat and stir in the lemon zest and juice and the basil. Serve immediately.

Kids' kedgeree

This yummy tea introduces kids to kedgeree without the need for the strong smoked-fish flavour and with only a little curry powder (fun for tiny taste buds).

What you need

350 g/12 oz **cod fillet**, skinned

300 ml/½ pint **whole milk**

50 g/1¾ oz **unsalted butter**

1 **onion**, finely chopped

½ teaspoon **cayenne pepper**

1 teaspoon **mild curry powder**

300 g/10½ oz **easy-cook long grain rice**

1 litre/1¾ pints reduced-salt **chicken stock** or water

150 g/5½ oz **frozen peas**, defrosted

150 g/5½ oz **frozen sweetcorn**, defrosted

4 **eggs**, hard-boiled and roughly chopped

2 tablespoons finely chopped **flat-leaf parsley**

What to do

1. Put the cod in a deep frying pan with the milk, bring to the boil, then reduce the heat to low and simmer uncovered for 5 minutes, or until cooked through.

2. Using a slotted spoon, transfer the fish to a bowl, reserving the warm milk. Flake the fish with a fork, taking care to remove any bones.

3. Melt the butter in a medium saucepan. Add the onion and cayenne pepper and cook for 2–3 minutes until the onion is beginning to soften. Add the curry powder and cook for a further minute.

4. Add the rice and stir to coat it in the oil. Pour in the chicken stock and the reserved milk and bring to the boil. Reduce the heat to low, cover and simmer for 10–15 minutes until the rice is cooked and almost all the stock and milk have been absorbed. Add the peas and the sweetcorn, stir thoroughly and cook for a further 2 minutes.

5. Carefully fold in the flaked fish and eggs. Sprinkle with the chopped parsley.

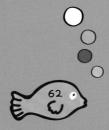

62

Ella's mum's easy chicken curry

serves **4** · prep **10** minutes · cook **30** minutes

Ella's mum first made this when Ella was just three years old – and Ella has been enjoying it ever since. It is a mild, sweet and creamy curry that's guaranteed to get tiny taste buds tingling with all the spices of exotic adventure.

What you need

2 tablespoons **olive oil**

1 small **onion**, chopped

2 **garlic** cloves, crushed

2 **chicken breasts** (about 300 g/10½ oz), cut into bite-sized pieces

2 cm/¾ inch piece **fresh ginger**, grated

1 teaspoon **mild curry powder**

1 small **sweet potato**, diced

250 g/9 oz **carrots**, sliced

250 ml/9 fl oz **light coconut milk**

100 ml/3½ fl oz reduced-salt **vegetable stock**

1 small **mango**, cut into chunks

125 g/4½ oz **green beans**, trimmed

2 tablespoons finely chopped **flat-leaf parsley**

What to do

1. Heat the oil in a large saucepan and add the onion and garlic. Fry for 1 minute, stirring, then add the chicken pieces and cook for 3–4 minutes over a medium heat, stirring every now and then until the chicken pieces are golden brown all over.

2. Add the grated ginger and the curry powder and cook for a further minute, stirring all the time. Add the sweet potato and carrots, then pour in the coconut milk and stock, and add the mango. Mix everything together well and bring the liquid to the boil. Cover, reduce the heat to low and simmer, stirring occasionally, for 20 minutes until the sweet potato is soft.

3. Add the beans and cook for a further 3 minutes until the beans are just soft. Finally, stir in the parsley. Serve immediately on a bed of rice or with a naan bread.

Ella's shortcut

To save some time on chopping, you can substitute a 90g/3¼ oz pouch of Ella's Kitchen Smoothie Fruits – The Yellow One for the chunks of mango.

Colour me in

64

Big beef ragù

This recipe came from a man called Neil who works at Ella's Kitchen selling our food in lots of countries around the world. He calls it the 'perfect pasta partner' and it packs a big taste punch. Go easy on the chilli flakes for very little ones.

What you need

1 tablespoon **olive oil**

½ **onion**, roughly chopped

1 **garlic** clove, sliced

25 g/1 oz **unsmoked back bacon**, chopped

300 g/10½ oz **lean minced beef**

500 g/1 lb 2 oz **passata** or **Clever Tomato Sauce** (see page 32)

1 tablespoon **Worcestershire sauce**

1 teaspoon **fennel seeds**

A pinch of **chilli flakes**

A few **basil** leaves, to serve (optional)

Parmesan cheese, grated, to serve (optional)

What to do

1. Heat the oil in a large saucepan and cook the onion and garlic over a moderate heat for 3–4 minutes until beginning to soften. Add the bacon and cook for 3 minutes until opaque. Add the minced beef and cook for a further 5 minutes until the mince has browned.

2. Pour in the passata or Clever Tomato Sauce and 50 ml/2 fl oz of water. Add the Worcestershire sauce and the herbs and spices. Bring the sauce to the boil, then reduce the heat to low, cover and simmer for 10 minutes. Remove the lid and stir and cook for a further 8–10 minutes until the liquid has reduced by almost half.

3. Serve the ragù over cooked pasta and sprinkle with basil leaves and freshly grated Parmesan (if using).

nee nar nee nar

67

Mega macaroni cheese

An easy twist on a family favourite, this dish is mega-tasty. The secret lies in the giant pasta tubes, which hold the delicious cheesiness so perfectly.

What you need

250 g/9 oz **large macaroni** or **penne pasta**, dried or fresh

100 g/ 3½ oz **butternut squash**, cut into small cubes

50 g/1¾ oz **unsalted butter**

50 g/1¾ oz **plain flour**

600 ml/1 pint **whole milk**

200 g/7 oz **Cheddar cheese**, grated

100 g/3½ oz **cauliflower florets**, grated

1 teaspoon **English** or **Dijon mustard**

A pinch of **ground nutmeg**

100 g/3½ oz **unsmoked back bacon**, grilled and chopped into pieces

Draw something for the digger to carry

What to do

1. Preheat the oven to 190°C/375°F/Gas Mark 5. Bring a large saucepan of lightly salted water to the boil and cook the pasta according to the packet instructions, adding the squash 5 minutes before the end of cooking. Drain and keep warm.

2. Meanwhile, melt the butter in a pan, add the flour, stir to combine and cook for 1 minute.

3. Gradually stir in the milk. Bring to the boil stirring continuously until the sauce thickens. Remove from the heat and stir in three-quarters of the Cheddar, the cauliflower, mustard, nutmeg and bacon pieces. Add the pasta and squash to the sauce and stir well.

4. Transfer the mixture to a large ovenproof dish and scatter with the remaining Cheddar.

5. Cook in the preheated oven for 20 minutes until golden.

6. Serve with green beans and a few grilled cherry tomatoes.

More veg!

Make your macaroni cheese more mega – try adding some of these veggies.

mmmmmmmmmmmacaroni

How does your fruit + veg grow?

Picking food out of the ground or off a tree helps children to get a proper sense of what food looks like before it arrives in the shops. Digging up potatoes makes for muddy fun; picking strawberries can turn fingers bright red. Scour your local paper and check online to see what pick-your-own possibilities there are near you.

① Go prepared

Make a date for the whole family to go picking together. Take gloves, wet-wipes, wellies and even a change of clothes – this could get grubby! Some pick-your-own farms have family centres where children can learn about the produce or see some animals.

What to choose?

Think about what works well for you all. Little ones will love picking strawberries, raspberries and peas, which grow low to the ground. Older children may like reaching for apples or pears from big trees in an orchard.

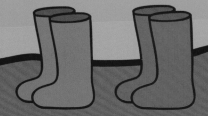

② Pick + talk

While you pick, talk about everything you can feel, see and smell. What does the earth feel like? What about the leaves? Are the fruit or veg you're picking hard or soft? How are they different from what you buy in the shops? Do they have a different smell? Perhaps they even look different. Talk about big and small. For potatoes, onions and large fruit, count them as you put them in the basket.

Go to market

If you can't go picking, visit a farmers' market, where the produce is fresh, fresh, fresh!

Heads up!

After apple or potato picking, try making your own fruit and veg heads. Cut out two eyes, a nose and a mouth from a magazine and stick them on. Add some wool or feathers for hair. Pom-poms with jewel stickers make gorgeous ears complete with earrings!

③ At home

Wash your booty together – who can scrub their potatoes cleanest? Taste the fruits as soon as you have washed them – deee-licious! Talk about your favourite ways to eat your hoard – then serve some of it up for tea. Yum!

Mmmmoussaka

serves 4 | prep 10 minutes | cook 50 minutes

Named after the sound little ones make when they eat it, this delicious dinner combines lamb mince with smooth sweet potato for a scrummy twist. Using crème fraîche instead of béchamel sauce saves you time without losing any creaminess.

What you need

2–3 tablespoons **olive oil**

½ **onion**, chopped (optional)

225 g/8 oz **lean minced lamb**

120 g/4¼ oz mashed **sweet potato**

1 small **aubergine**, sliced into rounds about 1 cm/½ in thick

1 large **potato**, sliced

100 g/3½ oz **Cheddar cheese**, grated

150 g/5½ oz **crème fraîche**

Blow!

What to do

1. Preheat the oven to 200°C/400°F/Gas Mark 6.

2. Heat 1 tablespoon of the oil in a saucepan, add the onion (if using) and cook for 3 minutes over a medium heat until softened. Add the mince and cook for 4–5 minutes, then reduce the heat, add the sweet potato mash and cook for a further minute. Remove from the heat; set aside.

3. Add the remaining oil to a large frying pan and gently fry the aubergine rounds for 10 minutes until soft.

4. Meanwhile, place the slices of potato in a large saucepan of water, bring to the boil, then reduce the heat to low and simmer uncovered for 10 minutes until the potatoes are slightly softened but not mushy.

5. In a shallow ovenproof dish, put a layer of meat mixture followed by a layer of both potato and aubergine. Repeat these layers, finishing with a neat layer of the potato and aubergine slices.

6. In a bowl mix three-quarters of the grated cheese with the crème fraîche. Spread this mixture over the top layer of the moussaka. Sprinkle over the remaining cheese, then cook in the oven for about 30 minutes until the top is golden and bubbling.

Ella's shortcut

To save having to mash up a sweet potato, try using a 120 g/4¼ oz pouch of Ella's Kitchen Sweet Potatoes, Broccoli + Carrots and you get the added benefit of more veggie goodness!

73

Totally cool Caribbean chicken with mango + pineapple

serves 6 · prep 15 minutes · cook 40 minutes

A flavour of the Caribbean makes this the most laid back of dinners. Watch it bring happy, sunny smiles to everyone at your table.

What you need

1 tablespoon **sunflower oil**

3 large **chicken breasts** (about 500 g/1 lb 2 oz), diced

1 **onion**, chopped

400 g/14 oz **potatoes**, diced

200 g/7 oz **butternut squash**, diced

1 teaspoon **medium curry powder**

½ teaspoon **ground cumin**

¼ teaspoon **ground cinnamon**

A pinch of **ground turmeric**

200 ml/7 fl oz reduced-salt **vegetable stock**

400 g/14 oz can **chopped tomatoes**

1 small, ripe **mango**, chopped into small pieces

100 g/3½ oz canned **pineapple chunks** in natural juice (drained weight)

What to do

1. Heat the oil in a large saucepan and fry the chicken and onion for 5 minutes until the onion is soft. Add the potato, squash and spices and cook for a further 4–5 minutes until the chicken is cooked through.

2. Add the vegetable stock and tomatoes to the pan and bring the sauce to the boil.

3. Stir in the chopped mango and the pineapple chunks, then reduce the heat to low, cover and simmer for 20 minutes, stirring occasionally. Remove the lid and cook for a further 10 minutes until the liquid has reduced to a thick sauce.

4. Serve immediately with rice.

Zingy lamb + couscous with mangoes + raisins

serves 6 · prep 15 minutes · cook 1¾ hours · omit green beans

Packed full of flavoursome fruit and veg, this couscous dish really does zing!

What you need

2 tablespoons **olive oil**

1 **garlic** clove, crushed

350 g/12 oz **lamb leg fillet**, diced

1 **onion**, chopped

2 teaspoons **ground cumin**

½ teaspoon **ground cinnamon**

1 **carrot**, diced

350 g/12 oz **butternut squash**, diced

400 g/14 oz can **chopped tomatoes**

500 ml/17 fl oz reduced-salt **vegetable stock**

1 small, ripe **mango**, chopped into small pieces

100 g/3½ oz **green beans**, cut into 1 cm/½ inch pieces

200 g/7 oz **couscous**

50 g/1¾ oz **raisins** (optional)

What to do

1. Preheat the oven to 180°C/350°F/Gas Mark 4.

2. Heat the oil in a frying pan and fry the garlic, lamb, onion and spices for 5 minutes until the lamb has browned on all sides. Transfer the mixture to a casserole dish.

3. Put the carrot and squash in the frying pan and cook for 3–4 minutes until softened, then add the tomatoes and 300 ml/½ pint of the stock and bring the mixture to the boil.

4. As soon as the tomato and stock mixture starts to boil, remove it from the heat and stir it into the lamb. Add the chopped mango, give it all another stir, then cover and bake in the oven for 1½ hours until the lamb is tender.

5. Once the lamb is ready, boil the green beans in the remaining stock for 2–3 minutes until just tender. Remove the beans from the liquid with a slotted spoon and set aside. Pour the stock into a measuring jug and set aside.

6. Put the couscous and raisins (if using) into a heatproof bowl and add the beans. Check how much stock you have in the measuring jug – you'll need 200 ml/7 fl oz, so top up with some boiling water if necessary. Pour the liquid over the couscous. Cover with clingfilm and leave for 5 minutes until absorbed. Fluff the couscous with a fork and serve with the lamb.

❄ The couscous is unsuitable for freezing, but pop the lamb into the freezer for another day.

Cosy cottage pie

Homely and hearty – even if you don't live in a cottage – this is always a favourite with little and big ones alike.

What you need

600 g/1 lb 5 oz **potatoes**, diced

50 ml/2 fl oz **whole milk**

200 g/7 oz **sweet potato**, diced

1 **carrot**, diced

1 **onion**, chopped

500 g/1 lb 2 oz **lean minced beef**

½ teaspoon **ground cinnamon**

250 ml/9 fl oz reduced-salt **vegetable stock**

2 **tomatoes**, chopped

100 g/3½ oz **frozen peas**, defrosted

What to do

1. Preheat the oven to 200°C/400°F/Gas Mark 6.

2. Cook the potatoes in boiling water for 10–15 minutes or until tender. Drain them and return them to the saucepan. Pour in the milk, then mash the potatoes well.

3. While the potatoes are bubbling, cook the sweet potato and carrot in another saucepan of boiling water for 10 minutes. Drain them and coarsely mash.

4. Fry the onion, minced beef and cinnamon for 5 minutes until the mince is completely brown. Add the stock, the mashed sweet potato and carrot mixture and the tomatoes to the mince and cook for 5 minutes. Add the peas, give it a stir and transfer it all to an ovenproof serving dish. Top with the mashed potato and bake in the oven for 30 minutes until golden.

Ella's shortcut

To save on some chopping time, replace the sweet potato and carrots with a 120 g/4¼ oz pouch of Ella's Kitchen Spinach, Apples + Swedes and reduce the amount of stock to 200 ml/7 fl oz.

Squishy salmon fishcakes

serves
2+2
adults + kids

prep
20
minutes
+ cooling

cook
25
minutes

omit
green
beans

Break out your artistic side and create lots of squishy fishy goodness
with lots of squishy fishy style.

What you need

400 g/14 oz **potatoes**, cut into
large dice

1 **carrot**, cut into small dice

200 g/7 oz **salmon fillets**,
skin removed

3 tablespoons **sunflower oil**

1 small **leek,** thinly sliced

25 g/1 oz **green beans,**
finely chopped

2 tablespoons finely chopped
flat-leaf parsley

Blowing bubbles

Turn the plate into a work of art –
ask your little one to arrange a few
peas as if the fishy fishcakes were
blowing bubbles.

What to do

① Cook the potato and carrot in boiling water
for 15 minutes until tender. Drain and mash
them together, then set aside to cool.

② Meanwhile, poach the salmon in simmering
water for 5 minutes until cooked through,
then lift out and allow to cool. Break the fish
into flakes, taking care to ensure that there are
no bones.

③ Heat 1 tablespoon of the oil in a large frying
pan and fry the leek and beans for 5 minutes
until tender. Stir them into the carrot and
potato mash, then add the cooked salmon
and the parsley to the mixture and stir again.

④ Using your hands, mould the mixture into
2 large fishcakes and 2 smaller fishcakes.
(Fishy shapes look great.)

⑤ Heat the remaining oil in a frying pan and
cook the fishcakes for 5 minutes, turning
once, until golden on both sides and heated
through. Serve immediately with some peas.

Colour us in

80

Crispy pork nuggets with apple mayo

Forget chicken, these golden pork nuggets taste fantastic, especially when served with this creamy twist on apple sauce.

What you need

2 **eggs**

1 teaspoon **dried thyme**

finely grated zest of 1 **lemon**

4 tablespoons **plain flour**

60 g/2¼ oz fresh white **bread-crumbs**, or **panko crumbs**

450 g/1 lb **lean pork fillet**, cut into about 12 slices, 2 cm-/¾ inch thick

Olive oil, for drizzling

Freshly ground **black pepper**

For the apple mayo

2 eating **apples**, peeled, cored and chopped

2 **garlic** cloves

4 tablespoons **mayonnaise**

1 teaspoon **olive oil**

Good squeeze of **lemon** juice

What to do

1. Preheat the oven to 200°C/400°F/Gas Mark 6. Line 2 baking trays with baking parchment.

2. Lightly beat the eggs in a small bowl and stir in the thyme and lemon zest. Put the flour in a separate bowl and season with pepper. Put the breadcrumbs or panko crumbs in a third bowl.

3. Dunk a pork slice in the flour, then in the egg mixture and finally in the breadcrumbs until coated all over. Place on a lined baking tray and repeat with the remaining pork and coatings.

4. Drizzle over a little oil and cook in the oven for 20–25 minutes, turning once, until golden and crisp on the outside and – when you cut into a big piece – the pork is not pink.

5. Meanwhile, make the apple mayo. Put the apples in a small saucepan with the garlic, add just enough water to cover, and cook for 5–8 minutes or until the apple is soft. Drain well.

6. Using a blender, blitz the apple and garlic with the mayonnaise, olive oil and lemon juice until smooth and creamy. To serve, dunk the pork nuggets into the apple mayo.

Wonderfully warming fruity beef stew

This is another of Ella's favourite meals – from her mum. Adding orange juice to the stew gives it a really fruity, tasty punch.

What you need

2 tablespoons **olive oil**

750 g/1 lb 10 oz **diced braising steak**

1 large **onion**, roughly chopped

200 g/7 oz **carrots**, thickly sliced

200 g/7 oz **swede**, peeled and cut into bite-sized chunks

2 **dried dates**, chopped (optional)

2 **garlic** cloves, chopped

1 teaspoon **dried thyme**

2 tablespoons **plain flour**

Juice and finely grated zest of ½ **orange**

700 ml/1¼ pints reduced-salt **beef stock**

Freshly ground **black pepper**

What to do

1. Preheat the oven to 160°C/325°F/Gas Mark 3.

2. Heat the oil in a large flameproof casserole dish over a medium-high heat. Add half the beef and cook for 5 minutes until browned on all sides. Remove with a slotted spoon and set aside in a bowl. Repeat with the remaining beef.

3. Reduce the heat to medium, add the onion, carrots and swede and cook with the lid on, stirring occasionally, for 5 minutes until softened. Add the dates (if using), garlic and thyme. Return the beef and all its juices to the casserole dish, add the flour and cook for 2 minutes, stirring continuously.

4. Add the orange zest, juice and beef stock. Season with pepper and bring to the boil.

5. Cover and put the casserole in the oven for 1¾–2 hours until the beef is tender, stirring halfway through and adding a splash of water if the sauce looks too dry. Serve with mashed potatoes, polenta, pasta or rice.

Scrummy salmon + veg parcels

makes **4** parcels · prep **10** minutes · cook **30** minutes

This is a fun way to cook simple, fresh ingredients. Wrapping the ingredients in shiny foil parcels makes them seem extra special.

What you need

Olive oil, for drizzling

300 g/10½ oz unpeeled **new potatoes**, thickly sliced

100 g/3½ oz **broccoli**, trimmed and halved

1 **red pepper,** deseeded and cut into thick strips

6 **baby sweetcorn**, halved lengthways

½ teaspoon **dried mixed herbs**

2 tablespoons **sun-dried tomato purée**

4 **salmon fillets**, skin removed

What to do

1. Preheat the oven to 200°C/400°F/Gas Mark 6.

2. Drizzle 4 large squares of aluminium foil with a little olive oil and make a small pile of the vegetable ingredients in the centre of each. Sprinkle each pile with some of the herbs.

3. Spread a ½ tablespoon of the tomato purée over each of the salmon fillets. Place 1 fillet on top of each pile of vegetables. Scrunch up the foil pieces, leaving a small gap in the top of each parcel to let the steam escape. Place the parcels on a baking sheet and bake in the oven for 30 minutes until the vegetables are tender and the salmon is cooked through.

Foil scrunch-up

Can I help?

Your children will love helping you construct the parcels – especially when it comes to scrunching up that noisy foil. Marvel together at how the contents have miraculously transformed when the parcels come out of the oven.

5 ways

Five ways with potatoes

Who knew potatoes could be so tasty? Gone are the days of bland school mash. Encourage little ones to make shapes from the potato peelings – or see who can peel the longest strip (under supervision, of course).

Rosemary roasties

serves 6 | prep 10 minutes | cook 1 hour

700 g/1 lb 9 oz **King Edward potatoes**, cut into large chunks

3 tablespoons **sunflower oil**

1 tablespoon **rosemary** leaves

Preheat the oven to 200°C/400°F/Gas Mark 6. Place the potatoes in a large saucepan, cover them with water, bring them to the boil, then reduce the heat to low and simmer for 10 minutes. Drain well and return the potatoes to the pan.

Add the oil and shake the pan a little to coat the potato cubes. Transfer them to a baking tray, drizzle over any excess oil left in the pan and sprinkle over the rosemary. Bake in the oven for 45–55 minutes until golden and crispy, turning the chunks after 30 minutes to make sure they go crispy all over.

Herby mash up

serves 6 | prep 10 minutes | cook 15 minutes

700 g/1 lb 9 oz **floury potatoes**, cut into chunks

50 g/1¾ oz **unsalted butter**

2 **garlic** cloves, crushed

50 ml/2 fl oz **whole milk**

2 tablespoons finely chopped **flat-leaf parsley**, or 4 tablespoons **crème fraîche** and 2 tablespoons chopped **chives** (optional)

Put the potatoes in a large saucepan, cover them with water, bring them to the boil, then reduce the heat to low and simmer for 10–15 minutes until tender. Drain well.

Put the empty pan back on the heat. Melt the butter and add the garlic, then fry it for 1 minute until soft. Remove the pan from the heat. Add the potatoes and the milk and mash well, then stir in the parsley.

Alternatively, mash the potatoes with the milk and stir in the crème fraîche and chopped chives in place of the parsley.

Baby jackets

700 g/1 lb 9 oz **new potatoes**

1 tablespoon **olive oil**

Preheat the oven to 200°C/400°F/Gas Mark 6.

Place the potatoes on a baking tray and sprinkle over the oil. Toss to coat evenly. Bake for 45 minutes or until golden and cooked all the way through.

Sweet potato fishy chips

700 g/1 lb 9 oz **sweet potatoes**, thickly sliced

1 tablespoon **sunflower oil**

2 tablespoons **maple syrup**

Preheat the oven to 200°C/400°F/ Gas Mark 6. Use a fish-shaped cutter to cut your sweet-potato slices into fishy chips. Put them in a large roasting tin, add the oil and maple syrup and toss to coat. Bake for 25–30 minutes until tender, turning once.

Cheesy chips

700 g/1 lb 9 oz **oven chips**

75 g/2½ oz **Cheddar cheese**, grated

Preheat the oven to 220°C/425°F/ Gas Mark 7. Spread the chips out on a large baking tray and cook for 20–25 minutes, or according to the packet instructions, until golden. Sprinkle over the Cheddar. Toss well until the cheese has melted slightly, then return to the oven for 1 minute.

Teeny-weeny burger bites

makes **6** | prep **35** minutes + proving | cook **20** minutes

These teeny-weeny turkey burgers are beautifully lean and just right for little hands to hold. If you can't find turkey mince, chicken mince will work just as well. We made our own rolls using pizza-base mix, but use shop-bought mini-burger rolls if you're short of time.

What you need

150 g/5½ oz **lean turkey mince**

25 g/1 oz fresh **white breadcrumbs**

2 **egg yolks**

A large pinch of **dried mixed herbs** or 2 teaspoons finely chopped fresh **oregano**

A splash of **Worcestershire sauce** (optional)

Flour, for dusting

2 teaspoons **vegetable oil**

Freshly ground **black pepper** (optional)

Slices of **tomato** and **cucumber**, to serve (optional)

For the rolls

145 g packet **pizza-base mix**

1 **egg**, beaten

Sesame seeds, for sprinkling

What to do

1. Preheat the oven to 220°C/425°F/Gas Mark 7. To make your mini rolls, make the pizza dough according to the packet instructions. Mould it into 6 pieces the size of ping-pong balls. Cover these with a damp cloth and leave to rise for 30 minutes, or until they have doubled in size. Place the rolls on a baking sheet and put them in the oven for 10 minutes, until they sound hollow when you tap the base. Remove them from the oven, brush them with the beaten egg, sprinkle over the sesame seeds and return to the oven for 2–3 minutes until they are golden on top.

2. While the rolls are baking, make the burgers. Mix the mince, breadcrumbs, egg yolks, herbs and Worcestershire sauce (if using) together in a bowl with a little freshly ground black pepper (if using), until the mixture is fully combined and moist, but holds together.

3. Divide the mixture into 6 equal portions, then flour your hands and roll each portion into a ball and gently flatten it into a burger shape.

4. Brush a nonstick frying pan with the oil, then put it on a low–medium heat and fry the burgers for 8–10 minutes, turning once, until they are completely cooked through.

5. Serve immediately in mini-burger buns topped and tailed with a slice of cucumber and a slice of tomato (if using).

❄ Freeze the burgers and buns separately.

Bite me

Quick quesadillas

serves 2 | prep 10 minutes | cook 20 minutes

Eat like a Mexican. We think these delicious quesadillas provide a perfect opportunity for a fiesta atmosphere – how about giving out some moustaches and party whistles?

What you need

1 tablespoon **olive oil**

1 **chicken breast** (about 150 g/5½ oz), sliced into strips

½ **red pepper**, deseeded and cut into thin strips

2 teaspoons **balsamic vinegar**

2 **flour tortillas**

1 tablespoon finely chopped **coriander**

50g/1¾ oz **Emmental** or **Cheddar cheese**, grated

What to do

1. Heat the oil in a frying pan and fry the chicken and pepper for 3–4 minutes, adding the balsamic vinegar for the final minute of cooking, until the chicken is cooked through and the pepper is soft.

2. Place a flour tortilla in the base of a separate frying pan and top with the cooked chicken and pepper, and the coriander. Sprinkle over the Emmental or Cheddar and top with the other tortilla.

3. Cover the pan with a lid and cook over a gentle heat for 12 minutes, or until the base of the tortilla is golden. Flip the tortilla over in the pan (you'll need 2 fish slices for this), and cook it for a further 1–2 minutes until the base is golden and the cheese has melted. Remove the tortilla from the pan and slice it into wedges.

4. Allow to cool slightly before serving.

Marvellous meatballs

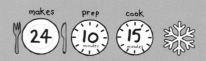

makes **24** · prep **10** minutes · cook **15** minutes

This basic mixture will make handfuls of meatballs that are ideal for play-date dinners. We've served them here with our Clever Tomato Sauce, but they're delicious inside our Pizza Pocket Bites (see page 153), too.

What you need

500 g/1 lb 2 oz **lean minced pork**

25 g/1 oz **breadcrumbs**

2 teaspoons **dried thyme**

2 teaspoons **Dijon mustard**

1½ teaspoons **Worcestershire sauce**

1 **garlic** clove, crushed

1 tablespoon **vegetable oil**

Freshly ground **black pepper**

What to do

1. Put the pork in a large mixing bowl and break it up using a fork. Stir in the rest of the ingredients, except the oil and pepper, first with a fork and then with your hands to mix everything together well. Season with black pepper and mix again.

2. Form the mixture into 24 mini meatballs, each about the size of a walnut.

3. Heat the oil in a large frying pan over a medium heat. Add the meatballs and fry for 15 minutes, reducing the heat to low if they start to become too dark, turning occasionally, until cooked through and golden. (You may need to do this in batches, in which case set each batch aside on a warm plate as it is cooked.)

4. Serve the meatballs on a mound of spaghetti topped with lashings of our Clever Tomato Sauce (see page 32).

❄ These meatballs can be frozen before or after they are cooked.

Three easy pasta sauces

These three pasta sauces are packed full of good, tasty stuff and can be stirred into any shape, size or colour of pasta. We've suggested which pasta to use, but why not try some different types, and see which you like best?

Lemony pea + mint pasta

serves 4–6 prep 10 minutes cook 15 minutes

What you need

1 tablespoon **olive oil**, plus extra for drizzling (optional)

1 large **onion**, chopped

1 **courgette**, chopped

200 g/7 oz **frozen peas**

2 **garlic** cloves, finely chopped

½ teaspoon low-salt **vegetable bouillon** powder

A handful of **mint leaves** (about 5 g/⅛ oz)

Squeeze of **lemon** juice

Freshly ground **black pepper**

Parmesan cheese, grated, to serve

8 cherry **tomatoes**, diced, to serve

What to do

1. Heat the olive oil in a large frying pan over a medium-low heat, add the onion and cook gently, stirring often, for 5 minutes. Add the courgette, peas and garlic and cook for another 10 minutes until softened.

2. Meanwhile, cook some conchiglie (shells) pasta according to the packet instructions.

3. Using a hand blender, blend the pea mixture with 150 ml/5 fl oz of the pasta cooking water (ladle it out as the pasta cooks), the bouillon powder and mint until smooth and creamy. Add a squeeze of lemon juice and season with pepper.

4. Serve the green sauce stirred into the pasta, topped with Parmesan, diced tomatoes and a final drizzle of olive oil, if you like.

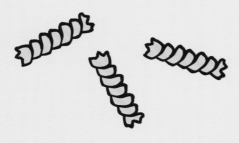

Turkey bolognese

serves 4–6 · prep 10 minutes · cook 35 minutes

What you need

2 tablespoons **olive oil**

1 large **onion**, finely chopped

1 **celery** stick, finely chopped

1 **carrot**, finely chopped

2 large **garlic** cloves, finely chopped

300 g/10½ oz **minced turkey**

1 teaspoon **dried oregano**

1 tablespoon **tomato purée**

400 g/14 oz can chopped **tomatoes**

185 ml/6 fl oz reduced-salt
  beef stock

Freshly ground **black pepper**

What to do

1. Heat the oil in a large saucepan over a medium heat. Add the onion and cook, stirring often, for 5 minutes. Reduce the heat slightly, add the celery and carrot and cook for another 5 minutes, covered, until the vegetables are tender.

2. Stir in the garlic and minced turkey and cook for 5 minutes, stirring to break up the meat, until it turns white and all trace of pink has gone.

3. Add the oregano, tomato purée, chopped tomatoes and stock and bring to the boil. Reduce the heat and simmer, part-covered with a lid, for 20 minutes, until the mince is cooked and the sauce has reduced and thickened. Season with pepper and serve over tagliatelle.

Big red tomato pesto

serves 4–6 · prep 15 minutes · cook 30 minutes

What you need

400 g/14 oz **tomatoes**, halved or quartered

4 **garlic** cloves, skins left on

2 tablespoons **extra virgin olive oil** (or oil from the jar of sun-dried tomatoes), plus extra for drizzling

25 g/1 oz **Brazil nuts**, roughly chopped

40 g/1½ oz **sun-dried tomatoes**, drained and roughly chopped

20 g/¾ oz **Parmesan** cheese, grated, plus extra for sprinkling

Freshly ground **black pepper**

Basil leaves, to serve

What to do

1. Preheat the oven to 200°C/400°F/Gas Mark 6. Put the tomatoes and garlic on a large baking tray and drizzle over a little olive oil. Toss well, then roast for 25–30 minutes until the tomatoes start to break down and the garlic is tender.

2. Finely chop the nuts in a food processor. Add the roasted tomatoes, dried tomatoes and oil. Squeeze each garlic clove out of its skin (discard the skin), add to the processor and blitz to a coarse paste. Season with pepper and stir in the Parmesan.

3. Cook some penne pasta according to the packet instructions. Stir 100 ml/3½ fl oz of the cooking water (ladle it out as the pasta cooks) into the pesto. Drain the pasta, return to the pan and stir in the pesto, some extra Parmesan and the basil leaves.

Lovely lasagne

serves 6   **prep** 20 minutes   **cook** 50 minutes

Loads of mums tell us that they avoid making lasagne because it takes so long to prepare. This version (and its veggie alternative) will take you only 20 minutes – easy peasy. Why not cook up a big batch and freeze it in portions?

What you need

1 **onion**, chopped

500 g/1 lb 2 oz **lean minced beef**

1 **carrot**, diced

200 g/7 oz **mushrooms**, sliced

1 teaspoon **dried mixed herbs**

½ teaspoon grated **nutmeg**

400 g/14 oz can **chopped tomatoes**

6 dried **lasagne sheets**

1 **egg**, beaten

200 g/7 oz **crème fraîche**

50 g/1¾ oz **Cheddar cheese**, grated

Go veggie

For a veggie option, fry the onion and carrot as in the meat version, then add 1 diced aubergine, 1 diced courgette and 150 ml/¼ pint reduced-salt vegetable stock. Add the mushrooms, herbs, nutmeg and tomatoes, cover the pan and simmer for 10 minutes, stirring occasionally. Continue as for the meat recipe from step 3 onwards.

What to do

1. Preheat the oven to 200°C/400°F/Gas Mark 6.

2. Fry the onion, mince and carrot in a large saucepan for 2–3 minutes until the mince is brown. Stir in the mushrooms, herbs, nutmeg, tomatoes and 150 ml/¼ pint water. Bring the sauce to the boil, then reduce the heat to low and simmer, covered, for 10 minutes, stirring occasionally.

3. Meanwhile, cook the lasagne sheets in boiling water for 5–6 minutes, drain, then cool.

4. Mix the egg with the crème fraîche.

5. Place a third of the mince mixture in the base of a shallow ovenproof dish, cover with 2 lasagne sheets and spoon over another third of the mince. Top with another 2 lasagne sheets and then the remaining mince mixture. Cover with the remaining lasagne sheets and pour over the crème fraîche and egg mixture. Finally, sprinkle over the Cheddar and bake in the oven for 30–35 minutes until the top is golden.

6. Serve warm with a salad.

Can I help?

Layer it up

Once cooled, parboiled lasagne sheets should be fairly robust for little hands to handle, so ask your toddler to help you make the layers: you do the meat and he or she does the lasagne. This way lasagne-making is a team effort!

99

Cool kiddie café

Children love to play at being grown-ups and what better way than to set up their own outdoor café in the garden. This is a great play-date activity, or a lovely way to involve the whole family in playing together. Of course, you can move the café inside on rainy days.

Today's specials

Make a menu

★ menu ★

Get creative with your menu. Find some paper, pens, stickers, glue and cut-outs of food from magazines and create a mouthwatering list of items that are on sale at your café.
Don't forget the tea, coffee and juices, too. If you have a wipe-clean drawing board or blackboard, you can create a specials list – let your little ones set the prices.

Pretend pizza

Try making pretend pizza slices out of cardboard – use differently coloured tissue paper for the toppings and cotton wool as melty cheese. If your customers demand pasta – no problem! Use a ball of yellow wool to make a bowl of delicious noodles.

2 Lay the table

Find a brightly coloured blanket or sheet to use as a tablecloth. If you don't have an outdoor table, make this a picnic café and lay your tablecloth on the ground, using cushions for seats. Are there any flowers you could pick in the garden to put in a little cup in the middle of the table? Give them a sniff – do they smell beautiful? Don't forget the plastic knives and forks and some tea-set cups and saucers.

3 Gather your food

Use playdough to make cakes or pretend sandwiches for your café; grass from the garden can make a pretend salad. You could also use real fruit, as well as water for tea and coffee.

4 Play your roles

Decide which of you will be the waiters, who will be the customers, and who will pretend to be the chef. Find aprons for the waiters and chef (who might need a hat, too, if you have one) and don't forget pen and paper to take orders. Show your customers to their seats and hand them their menus. What do the customers think of the food?

Teatime treat

When the game is over, keep the outdoor café and serve up proper tea there for your little ones. They will love it when you are the waiter or waitress serving real food in their café – will they leave you a tip?!

Full-of-sunshine Thai curry

serves 4 | prep 10 minutes | cook 18 minutes

Bursting with bright colours, this gentle introduction to Thai flavours provides plenty of adventure for tiny taste buds.

What you need

1 tablespoon **vegetable oil**

400 g/14 oz **butternut squash**, diced

1 large **onion**, diced

1 **carrot**, sliced

1 **red pepper**, deseeded and sliced

100 g/3½ oz **sugar snap peas**

3 cm/1¼ inch piece **root ginger**, grated

1 **garlic** clove, crushed

1 teaspoon **ground cumin**

½ teaspoon **mild chilli powder**

400 ml/14 fl oz can **coconut milk**

1 reduced-salt **vegetable stock cube**, crumbled

A large handful of **coriander**, finely chopped

4 **lime** wedges, to serve (optional)

What to do

1. Heat the oil in a large frying pan and cook the squash, onion and carrot for 5 minutes unil the onion is soft. Add the pepper, sugar snap peas, ginger, garlic and spices and fry for 2–3 minutes, stirring occasionally.

2. Stir in the coconut milk and crumbled stock cube, cover and simmer for 10 minutes, stirring occasionally, until the vegetables are tender. Stir in the coriander.

3. Serve the curry with basmati rice, and lime wedges (if using).

Thai-taste-tastic!

Thai food is famously fragrant, which makes this a fab meal for encouraging your toddler to explore how smell and taste work together. Offer up the cut ginger root and a few coriander leaves for a sniff-fest. Talk about the different smells. Can your toddler taste those smells when he or she tucks into the bowl of cooked curry?

Splish Splash Salmon Fajitas

serves **2+2** adults + kids

prep **20** minutes

cook **20** minutes filling only

Fun and colourful, these fajitas are filled with healthy salmon and lots of fresh veg. For a super-quick version, you can use ready-cooked salmon (just leave out the fajita spices).

What you need

1½ teaspoons **fajita seasoning mix**

Juice of 2 **limes**

450 g/1 lb **salmon fillet**

3–4 **soft tortillas**

1 large ripe **avocado**

2 teaspoons **olive oil**

3–4 tablespoons **soured cream**, or **Greek yogurt** (optional)

For the mango salsa

1 large cob fresh **sweetcorn**

1 **red pepper**, deseeded and quartered

1 **spring onion**, roughly chopped

100 g/3½ oz **mango**, cut into small pieces

A handful of **coriander,** chopped (optional)

Taco-tastic

Instead of salmon, try mackerel fillets, thick fillets of white fish such as cod or haddock, or even tiger prawns cooked in garlic butter. Leftover roast chicken or pork slices make great substitutes for fish too, and will use up the last of a roast in a creative way.

What to do

1. In a small bowl, mix together the fajita seasoning with the juice of 1 lime. Rub the mixture into the flesh side of the salmon, cover and set aside while you make the salsa.

2. Stand the corn cob on its end and slice off the kernels. Heat a large, dry frying pan over a medium heat, add the corn kernels and cook for 5 minutes, turning occasionally, until softened and starting to colour – take care, as they start to pop. Transfer to a bowl.

3. Add the red pepper and spring onion to the dry pan. Cook for 5 minutes, turning once, until they start to char. Remove from the pan and finely chop, then add to the corn with the mango and the coriander (if using). Add the juice of half a lime and set aside.

4. Preheat the oven to 180°C/350°F/Gas Mark 4. Wrap the tortillas in foil and warm in the oven until needed.

5. In a separate bowl, mash the avocado flesh with the remaining lime juice.

6. Add a splash of olive oil to the frying pan and cook the salmon for 4–5 minutes on each side, or until just cooked through. Remove from the pan, peel away the skin and flake the salmon into pieces.

7. To assemble, spoon some mashed avocado onto each warmed tortilla, top with the flaked salmon and some salsa. Finish with a spoonful of soured cream or yogurt, if you like. The tortillas can be folded, rolled or served flat – whichever way, napkins are a must!

Perfect puds

Have you tried the Swirly Whirly Cheesecake? It's my favourite!

Love, Ella x

Baby baked apples

A favourite winter pud, the mini apples are filled with a cinnamon and fruit butter, then baked until lovely and soft.

What you need

60 g/2¼ oz stoned **dates**

8 mini eating **apples**, washed and dried

50 g/1¾ oz **unsalted butter,** softened

1 teaspoon **ground cinnamon**

1 teaspoon **vanilla extract**

40 g/1½ oz **raisins**

Juice of ½ **orange**

Squeeeezy juicy

> Can I help?

Whether you have a citrus press or a hand citrus juicer, pressing down on the flesh of the orange and watching the delicious juice come out is pure culinary magic for little ones. Put the juice in a measuring jug to see how much you managed to squeeze out.

What to do

1. Put the dates in a small heatproof bowl. Pour over enough just-boiled water from a kettle to cover, then leave to soak for 20 minutes until softened. Drain the dates, throwing away the soaking water, then chop them.

2. Preheat the oven to 180°C/350°F/Gas Mark 4. Cut a triangular-shaped cavity from each apple, removing most of the core at the same time but keeping the bottom intact. Cut a sliver from the base if the apples won't stand up, then score around the circumference with a sharp knife to stop them splitting.

3. Using a hand blender, blend the butter, chopped dates, cinnamon and vanilla until combined. Stir in the raisins. Fill each of the apples with the raisin butter, pressing the mixture into the cavities.

4. Place the apples in a baking dish, spoon over the orange juice and cover with foil. Bake for 40 minutes until the apples are soft but not collapsing, removing the foil halfway through to spoon over the buttery juices in the tin. Serve with spoonfuls of crème fraîche or Greek yogurt.

Scrummy

What shapes can you make?

Toasty, fruity brioche

 serves **6** prep **10** minutes cook **20** minutes

Orange-coloured fruit such as peaches, mangoes and apricots – fresh or tinned – work best for this scrummy dessert. Serve it plain or with Greek yogurt or crème fraîche. If you prefer, you can swap the brioche for croissants.

What you need

25 g/1 oz **unsalted butter**, softened

6 slices **brioche**

2 tablespoons **apricot jam**

1 **mango** or 6 **apricots** or 2 **nectarines** or 2 **peaches** or a mixture of any, stoned and sliced

1 tablespoon **soft brown sugar**

4 tablespoons freshly squeezed **orange juice**

What to do

1. Preheat the oven to 200°C/400°F/Gas Mark 6. Butter each slice of brioche, then place the slices in a baking dish so that they fit snugly. Spread them with the apricot jam.

2. Place the sliced fruit on top of the brioche until the brioche is completely covered and you have used up all the fruit.

3. Sprinkle over the sugar and drizzle over the orange juice so that the brioche is moist.

4. Bake the pudding in the oven for 20 minutes until the brioche is slightly crisped and browned at the edges. Serve hot.

Fruity fun

Can I help?

In creating this recipe, the children can have all the creative fun – putting the fruit on top of the jammy brioche slices and making a pattern on top. Lay out the slices of fruit for them and away they go!

Colour me in

111

Big banana + honey dream

A match made in heaven, banana and honey make a dreamy combination that wraps a warm hug around the taste buds.

What you need

150 ml/¼ pint **whipping cream**

3 ripe **bananas**

250 ml/9 fl oz **Greek yogurt**

2 tablespoons **clear honey**

1 tablespoon **lemon juice**

Chocolate buttons or juicy **mango** slices, to decorate

What to do

1. Whip the cream until soft peaks form. Mash the bananas on a plate and then transfer them to a bowl.

2. Stir the yogurt, honey and lemon juice into the banana, then gently fold in the whipped cream.

3. Spoon the mixture into 6 individual serving dishes and decorate with the chocolate buttons or mango slices.

Causing a stir

Can I help?

Tiny tots will love having a turn at whipping the cream and stirring the mixture all together. Chocolate buttons or mango on top – the results are always irresistible!

Fruity granola crisp

serves
6
Granola serves 8

prep
15 minutes

cook
40 minutes

Here, you get two recipes in one…a delicious fruity compote and a crispy granola topping, both cooked in the oven. Store any leftover granola in a jar to serve as a yummy breakfast tomorrow, with yogurt.

What you need

For the granola

85 g/3 oz **jumbo porridge oats**

20 g/¾ oz **sunflower seeds**

1 tablespoon **sesame seeds**

50 g/1¾ oz **pecan nuts**, roughly chopped

1 teaspoon **ground cinnamon**

1½ tablespoons **coconut oil**

35 g/1¼ oz **runny honey**

For the compote

300 g/10½ oz **frozen raspberries**

4 ripe **pears**, peeled, cored and cut into bite-sized chunks

Juice of 1 large **orange**

1 teaspoon **vanilla** extract

A little honey, if needed

What to do

1. Preheat the oven to 160°C/325°F/Gas Mark 3. Line a large baking tray with baking parchment.

2. To make the granola, mix the oats, sunflower seeds, sesame seeds, pecans and ground cinnamon in a large mixing bowl. Gently heat the coconut oil and honey in a small saucepan over a low heat, pour over the oat mixture and stir well until combined.

3. Tip the granola mix onto the prepared tray, spread into an even layer and bake for 40 minutes, turning halfway through, until crisp and golden. Leave to cool slightly and crisp up further – you can roughly chop it if you want a finer mixture for small children.

4. For the compote, mix all the ingredients in an ovenproof dish and place in the oven to cook at the same time as the granola topping. Cook for 35–40 minutes, stirring halfway through, until the pears are tender. Taste and sweeten with a little honey if it's too tart.

5. Serve the fruit compote with a sprinkling of granola on top.

 Freeze the fruit compote only.

Go nuts!

As long as you stick to the same amounts given in the recipe, you can switch the nuts and seeds, adding your favourites, or whatever you've got in the cupboard. Try chopped Brazil nuts instead of pecans, or swap in pumpkin seeds for sunflower seeds.

Mmmminty green lollies

No one will guess the secret ingredient in these refreshing, creamy lollies. Make sure the avocado (shhh!) and bananas are perfectly ripe for the best flavour. If not using peppermint extract, add an extra tablespoon of finely chopped mint leaves, though the lollies won't be quite so minty.

What you need

1 ripe **avocado**

2 ripe **bananas**, peeled and sliced

⅓ teaspoon pure **peppermint extract,** or to taste (optional)

200 ml/7 fl oz **coconut water**

1 tablespoon finely chopped **mint leaves**, plus extra if needed

1 tablespoon runny **honey**, or to taste

Juice of 2 **limes**

What to do

1. Halve the avocado, take out the stone, then scoop the flesh into a blender.

2. Add the bananas plus all the other ingredients and blend until smooth and creamy. If you didn't use peppermint extract, add an extra tablespoon of finely chopped mint leaves.

3. Taste and make sure you are happy with the level of sweetness and minty flavour, adding more honey or peppermint extract if you want. When frozen, the flavours in the mixture will be muted, so be brave!

4. Pour the mixture into 6 lolly moulds and freeze for at least 6 hours, or preferably overnight, until firm.

117

Playing shops

Creating your own shop together is a perfect opportunity for play involving all five senses. A greengrocer's shop is a great way to start and will fire your children's imaginations to think about the fruit and veg they so often see at mealtimes. Keep it varied by using different 'goods' each time you play.

1

Make your signage

Every shop needs an open and closed sign. Grab some card (the inside of an old cereal box will do) and get creative. You can write the word, but let the little hands do the decorating.

Make a kiosk

Take a large cardboard box (big enough for a little face to appear in), then use a craft knife to cut a flap for the shop window where goods and play cash change hands. Together, decorate the outside of the kiosk with lettering and stickers and make a sign that says 'Pay here'.

2

Choose your stock

It's time to raid the fridge! Borrow a few tomatoes, carrots and onions, and any other vegetables that your toddler wants you to sell in the store. Don't forget the fruit and herbs, too. Talk about the colours, smells and textures. Remember to get out the weighing scales!

Use some play money, or make some out of coloured paper rectangles and cardboard circles. Don't forget to give change!

3

Make a display

Group your chosen foods together – will you arrange them by colour or by type? Count how many different kinds of food you have. Make the display look beautiful. You might, for example, set it out like a rainbow, or lay the foods out like a face, a train, or some other shape. Decorate little labels to put next to each item. How much does everything cost?

4

Go shopping

You start off as the shopkeeper and ask your toddler to visit with a favourite toy. Ask them to bring a shopping bag or basket. What would they like to buy today? Encourage them to 'try before you buy' so they even get to taste the products, too.

50p

£1.50
10p

Swirly whirly cheesecake

This is everyone's favourite dessert – it's a delicious sweet treat with no added sugar.

What you need

100 g/3½ oz **dates**, stoned

50 g/1¾ oz **roasted hazelnuts**

100 g/3½ oz **oatcakes**, broken up

50 g/1¾ oz **unsalted butter**, melted

2 teaspoons **cornflour**

375g/13 oz **strawberries**, hulled and puréed, plus extra to serve

400 g/14 oz **cream cheese**

2 teaspoons **vanilla extract**

300 ml/½ pint thick **Greek yogurt** or **half-fat crème fraîche** (or use half and half)

Marble-ous!

Can I help?

Try out your tot's artistic talents by asking her or him to have a go at making the swirly whirly marbling pattern on top of the cheesecake.

Ella's shortcut

You can sidestep making the strawberry purée by substituting 2 x 90 g/ 3¼ oz pouches of Ella's Kitchen Smoothie Fruits – The Red One.

What to do

1. Put the dates in a small heatproof bowl and pour over enough just-boiled water to cover. Soak for 20 minutes until softened. Drain, then whiz to a paste with a hand blender.

2. Line the base of a 20 cm/8 inch loose-based cake tin with baking parchment. Blitz the hazelnuts and oatcakes for a few seconds in a food processor until they have the texture of breadcrumbs. Spoon into a mixing bowl. Add half the dates and all the melted butter and stir until combined. Spoon into the cake tin and press down with the back of a spoon until firm. Chill in the fridge until needed.

3. Meanwhile, stir the cornflour into a small amount of the strawberry purée. Heat the rest of the strawberry purée and the remaining dates in a small saucepan over a medium-low heat. Stir in the strawberry-cornflour mixture and cook, stirring often, for about 10 minutes, or until reduced and thickened. Leave to cool.

4. Whisk the cream cheese in a large bowl with the vanilla and yogurt and/or crème fraîche until thick and creamy, then stir in half the strawberry purée. Remove the base from the fridge and spoon the topping over.

5. To decorate, drizzle over half the remaining strawberry purée in a spiral, starting from the centre, then run a skewer through the spiral to get a marbled effect. Pour the rest of the purée into a jug and set aside.

6. Chill the cheesecake for at least 2 hours, or longer if time allows, to firm up. Serve with strawberries and the extra purée on the side.

Strawberry mush up

This is a bit like Eton mess, but much easier to put together. Ripe juicy strawberries, cool creamy yogurt and crunchy sweet meringue pieces create a festival of taste and texture. If you like, you can drizzle extra strawberry purée on top and decorate with a few extra berries.

What you need

3 ready-made **meringue** nests
(or make your own, see below)

300 g/10½ oz **strawberries**,
chopped, plus a further
150 g/5½ oz fresh or frozen
strawberries, puréed

200 ml/7 fl oz **Greek yogurt**

What to do

1. Use your hands to break the meringue nests into small pieces in a large mixing bowl. Add the chopped strawberries, reserving a few for decoration, and stir in the yogurt.

2. Add 2 tablespoons of puréed strawberries and stir through gently to make the mixture streaky.

3. Spoon the mixture into 6 glasses or bowls and decorate with a few strawberry pieces and an extra drizzle of purée if you have it. Serve while the meringue is still crunchy.

Make your meringue

To make your own meringues, preheat the oven to 110°C/225°F/Gas Mark ½. Whisk 3 egg whites until stiff, then whisk in 175 g/6 oz caster sugar, a teaspoon at a time. Whisk until the meringue is thick and glossy. Mix 1 teaspoon each of cornflour and white wine vinegar with ½ teaspoon vanilla extract, and whisk this into the meringue. Spoon the mixture into 8 mounds on a parchment-lined baking sheet and bake for 1½–1¾ hours. Keep the leftovers for another day!

Ella's shortcut

If you prefer, you can replace the strawberry purée with 2 tablespoons of Ella's Kitchen Smoothie Fruits – The Red One.

Creamy coconut rice pudding with chunky mango sauce

A very nice lady called Cath does all the sums at Ella's Kitchen. She's also a bit of a pudding queen and has created this variation on a traditional rice pud.

What you need

20 g/¾ oz **unsalted butter**

120 g/4¼ oz **pudding rice**

50 g/1¾ oz **soft light brown sugar**

400 ml/14 fl oz can **light coconut milk**

800 ml/1¼ pints **whole milk**

2 teaspoons **vanilla extract**

½ teaspoon **ground cinnamon**

For the mango sauce

1 small, ripe **mango**, chopped

A squeeze of **lime juice**

What to do

1. Preheat the oven to 150°C/300°F/Gas Mark 2 and grease an ovenproof pudding dish (30 x 20 cm/12 x 8 inches) with a little of the butter.

2. Spread the rice evenly over the base of the pudding dish. Sprinkle the sugar on top.

3. Pour the coconut milk into a separate bowl and use a balloon whisk to mix it up thoroughly. Add the milk, vanilla extract and cinnamon and mix again.

4. Pour the coconut milk mixture over the rice and sugar and dot the top with the remaining butter. Put the dish in the centre of the oven and bake for 2–2½ hours until the top is golden brown.

5. While the pudding is cooking, prepare the mango sauce. Using a hand blender, purée three-quarters of the mango and a squeeze of lime juice until smooth. Dice the remaining mango and stir it into the purée.

6. Serve the rice pudding hot or cold with the mango sauce spooned on top.

Classroom kitchen

Ask your little helpers to taste a spoon of coconut milk and then a spoon of whole milk. Talk about the different tastes they have and the different places that they come from.

Berry nice blueberry cream

Blueberries proved a definite hit with our pint-sized tasters. You can also make this fuss-free, creamy sundae for breakfast, if you prefer.

What you need

200 ml/7 fl oz **half-fat crème fraîche**

300 ml/½ pint **Greek yogurt**

Juice and finely grated zest of 1 **lemon**

300 g/10½ oz **blueberries**

1 tablespoon **clear honey**

Icing sugar, for dusting

What to do

1. Put the crème fraîche in a mixing bowl with the Greek yogurt and fold through the grated lemon zest. Divide a third of the mixture between 4 serving dishes.

2. Reserve a few blueberries for decoration. Put the remaining blueberries into a bowl with 1 tablespoon of lemon juice and the honey. Lightly mash with a potato masher, just until a few blueberries have burst, but most still remain whole. Stir well.

3. Divide half the blueberry mixture between the dishes in an even layer on top of the crème fraîche. Top with a further third of the crème fraîche mixture, the remaining blueberry mixture, and finally the last third of the crème fraîche.

4. Decorate the top of the sundae with a few of the reserved blueberries and dust with icing sugar to serve.

    Pop this in the freezer and you will end up with ice cream!

One for you

One for me

Smiley spiral apple tarts

makes **6** | prep **20** minutes | cook **15–20** minutes

Who knew apple tarts could taste this good? Little ones will love to get involved using pastry cutters and decorating the tarts with apple slices.

What you need

320 g/11¼ oz ready-made **puff pastry**

2 eating **apples** (Granny Smith or Royal Gala work best)

1 tablespoon **lemon juice**

50 g/1¾ oz **unsalted butter**, cut into 6 cubes

½ teaspoon **ground cinnamon**

25 g/1 oz **soft light brown sugar**

Roll, cut, fill

Can I help?

Tots of all ages get to play at being baker with these simple apple tarts. Making them is a brilliant activity for a play date. One friend rolls the dough, another cuts the circles and another fills the tart with pieces of apple.

What to do

1. Preheat the oven to 200°C /400°F/Gas Mark 6.

2. Roll out the puff pastry until it is 5 mm/¼ in thick. Using a 10 cm/4 inch pastry cutter, stamp out 6 circles and place them, spaced well apart, on a baking sheet.

3. Peel, quarter and core the apples, then cut them into very thin slices. Place them in a bowl with the lemon juice and toss well to coat them in the juice. Arrange the apple slices on top of the dough circles in a 'flower' pattern.

4. Place a cube of butter in the centre of each circle, then sprinkle with a little cinnamon (to taste) and the sugar.

5. Bake in the oven for 15–20 minutes until golden brown. Serve the tarts warm or cold with vanilla ice cream or crème fraîche.

Wonderful watermelon ice

A kind of kiddie granita, this is the ultimate zingy-fresh slushie. The freezing and scraping process to make the ice slush is all part of the fun.

What you need

900 g/2 lb **watermelon** flesh, cubed (about a 1.8 kg/4 lb watermelon, seeds removed)

50 g/1¾ oz **caster sugar**

Juice of 1 **lime**

Get ahead

You can make this icy pudding up to 3 days before you need it. Keep it in the freezer with the lid on the container, or tightly covered with foil. Then, when you're ready, give it a quick scrape and a mash with a fork before serving.

Save the seeds!

Don't throw away the seeds from your watermelon – dried-out seeds are brilliant for making shakers or using as 'money' in a game of shops. Rinse the discarded seeds in water, then lay them out on kitchen paper in a warm place for 7–10 days. The seeds are completely dry when they snap rather than bend between your fingers.

What to do

1. Put all the ingredients in a food processor and whiz until smooth (you can put everything in a bowl and use a hand blender if you don't have a food processor).

2. Pour the mixture into a shallow freezer-proof container, put the lid on and freeze the mixture for 1 hour.

3. Remove the mixture from the freezer and stir it well, mashing any frozen parts with the back of a fork.

4. Replace the lid and freeze the mixture for a further 2 hours until firm.

5. Using a fork, scrape the frozen mixture vigorously to form icy flakes. Serve in plastic cups or small glasses.

Colour me in

Zingy pineapple with basil + lime

These ingredients sound quite grown up, but we've found that older toddlers are interested to find out about the zesty tastes and textures – and then love them when they tuck in.

What you need

Juice and finely grated zest of 1 **lime**

50 g/1¾ oz **soft dark brown sugar**

1 tablespoon finely chopped **basil** leaves

1 whole **pineapple**, peeled, cored and cut into 'soldier'-like slices

What to do

1. Place the lime zest and juice in a bowl and stir in the sugar and basil. Leave the mixture to marinate for 5 minutes until the sugar has dissolved to form a syrup.

2. Arrange the pineapple 'soldiers' on a large serving plate and drizzle over some of the lime and basil syrup. Put any remaining syrup in a little bowl for extra dunking. Serve immediately.

Smell-a-thon

Crushing the basil releases its delicious smell – talk to your toddler about it and what it might remind you of. Summertime? Pizza? And what about the smell of the lime? How is that different from the pineapple?

Make it mango

As an alternative, you can replace the pineapple with 2 peeled and sliced fresh mangoes for a different kind of tropical flavour.

132

Fabulous fruit compote

serves 8 · prep 10 minutes · cook 20 minutes

You can enjoy this versatile fruit compote for breakfast served with yogurt and granola, as a hot or cold snack, or for a dinnertime pud served with ice cream or custard.

What you need

2 eating **apples**, peeled, cored and diced

2 **Conference pears**, peeled, cored and diced

350 g/12 oz **plums**, stoned and diced

75 g/2½ oz **dried prunes**, roughly chopped

50 g/1¾ oz **sultanas**

Juice and finely grated zest of 1 **orange**

½ teaspoon **ground mixed spice**

What to do

1. Place all the ingredients in a medium saucepan, cover with a lid and cook gently for 20 minutes, stirring occasionally, until the fruit has softened but there is still some texture.

2. Remove the pan from the heat. Serve the compote warm or cold.

Hello...

Scrummy treats

Hello!
How many bananas
can you spot in
this chapter?
Love, Ella x

Teeny weeny fruit muffins

makes 12 · prep 15 minutes · cook 35 minutes

The fruit purée makes these muffins reeeally moist. They are easy peasy to make and bake in 20 minutes, so they provide a perfect afternoon cooking activity when a friend comes to play. Mmmm…warm muffins to keep them going until tea. Perfect!

What you need

75 g/2½ oz **unsalted butter**

75 g/2½ oz **strawberries**, hulled

125 g/4½ oz **bananas** (about 2) sliced

1 **egg**

1 teaspoon **vanilla extract**

100 g/3½ oz **self-raising wholemeal flour**

¾ teaspoon **baking powder**

50 g/1¾ oz **raisins**

40 g/1½ oz **walnuts**, chopped (optional)

Porridge oats, for sprinkling

What to do

1. Preheat the oven to 180°C/350°F/Gas Mark 4. Line a mini muffin tin with paper cake cases.

2. Melt the butter in a small saucepan, then leave to cool slightly.

3. Using a hand blender, whiz the strawberries and bananas together in a bowl until almost smooth.

4. Pour the fruit purée into a mixing bowl and beat in the melted butter, the egg and vanilla. Sift in the flour and baking powder and stir again. Finally, stir in the raisins and walnuts (if using).

5. Divide the mixture between the cake cases, filling each one three-quarters full so that the muffins have room to rise. Sprinkle a few porridge oats over each muffin.

6. Bake for 30–35 minutes, or until the muffins are firm to the touch and golden on top. Cool on a wire rack before serving. They will keep in an airtight container for up to 3 days.

Bake away!

Can I help?

This is a baking extravaganza for tiny helpers. Little ones can get stuck in with the egg-cracking, the sifting, the stirring and the sprinkling – so much to do, so much messy fun to be had.

Rise 'n' shine banana bread

makes **10** slices · prep **10** minutes · cook **40** minutes

This simple banana bread is deliciously moist and ideal for a late breakfast, as a snack for a trip to the park, or with a cup of juice mid-afternoon.

What you need

310 g/11 oz ripe **bananas**, mashed

2 tablespoons **agave syrup**

3 **eggs**

250 g/9 oz **self-raising flour**

1 teaspoon **baking powder**

1 teaspoon **bicarbonate of soda**

25 g/1 oz **butter**, cubed

What to do

1. Preheat the oven to 160°C/325°F/Gas Mark 3. Lightly oil a 900 g/2 lb loaf tin.

2. Put the mashed banana, agave syrup and eggs in a bowl and use a wooden spoon to beat them together until well combined.

3. In a separate large bowl, sift together the flour, baking powder and bicarbonate of soda, then use your fingertips to rub in the butter until the mixture resembles fine breadcrumbs.

4. Tip the egg and banana mixture into the dry ingredients and mix them together until well combined. Spoon the mixture into the prepared loaf tin and level the top. Bake for 1–1¼ hours until well risen and golden, and hollow-sounding when you tap the base.

5. Cool the loaf in the tin, then turn it out and cut into slices to serve.

141

Choccie chocolate munchies

This is a fave with all little cookie monsters and there's no baking required, which means that they can get involved in every stage of the making…as well as the eating!

What you need

50 g/1¾ oz stoned **dates**

50 g/1¾ oz **pecan nuts**

100 g/3½ oz **unsalted butter**, melted, plus extra for greasing

165 g/5¾ oz **digestive biscuits**

1 small ripe **avocado**, mashed

2 tablespoons **cocoa powder**

50 g/1¾ oz **raisins**

1 tablespoon ground **flaxseeds/ linseeds** (optional)

100 g/3½ oz **dark chocolate**, broken into pieces

Munchie making

Can I help?

Get your little ones involved in the biscuit bashing in this recipe. Ask for help breaking up, melting and pouring over the chocolate, too.

What to do

1. Put the dates in a small heatproof bowl and pour over enough just-boiled water to cover. Soak for 20 minutes until softened.

2. Meanwhile, toast the pecans in a large dry frying pan for 4 minutes, turning once, until they start to brown. Tip the pecans onto a plate, leave to cool, then break into pieces.

3. Line the bottom of a 20 cm/8 inch square baking tin with baking parchment and grease the sides with butter. Put the biscuits in a bowl (or freezer bag) and bash with the end of a rolling pin until broken into uneven pieces. Tip into a large mixing bowl.

4. Drain the dates and put them in a blender with the avocado, melted butter and cocoa powder and blend until smooth.

5. Spoon the mixture into the bowl with the biscuits, then add the pecans, raisins and ground flaxseeds (if using) and stir well. Spoon the mixture into the tin and press down firmly with the back of the spoon. Place in the fridge while you prepare the chocolate.

6. Melt the chocolate in a heatproof bowl over a pan of simmering water (or melt in a microwave on medium for 2–3 minutes). Remove the biscuit mixture from the fridge and spread the melted chocolate over. Return to the fridge for another hour or until set.

7. Remove from the fridge and cut the chocolate munchies into 16 pieces. Store in an airtight container in the fridge for up to 1 week.

Super seedy crackers

serves 20 | prep 10 minutes + resting | cook 45 minutes

Bursting with good things, this handy, easy, mega-crunchy snack
will keep in an airtight tin for up to five days.

What you need

70 g/2½ oz **pumpkin seeds**,
roughly chopped

70 g/2½ oz **sunflower seeds**,
roughly chopped

70 g/2½ oz **sesame seeds**

2 tablespoons ground **flaxseeds/
linseeds**

50 g/1¾ oz **chia seeds**

175 g/6 oz **porridge oats**

1 tablespoon runny **honey**

3 tablespoons **olive oil**, or
coconut oil

½ teaspoon **sea salt** (optional)

Mix it up!

There's no end to the ways you can vary
these wonderfully adaptable crackers.
Try adding: ¾ teaspoon ground
cinnamon for a biscuit bite; 2 sun-dried
tomatoes, finely chopped, for a savoury
tang; 1 small carrot, finely grated, for
sweetness; 1 teaspoon of your favourite
spice mix, for spiciness; or even 2
tablespoons nutritional yeast flakes
instead of the ground flaxseeds/linseeds,
for a 'cheesy' though dairy-free taste.

What to do

1. Put the pumpkin, sunflower and sesame
   seeds, ground flaxseeds, chia seeds and oats
   in a large mixing bowl.

2. Pour in 300 ml/10½ fl oz water and stir well.
   Leave to sit for 30 minutes to let the chia
   seeds expand and turn jelly-like in texture.

3. Preheat the oven to 190°C/375°F/Gas Mark 5.
   Line 2 large baking sheets with baking
   parchment.

4. Gently warm the honey and oil in a small
   saucepan over a low heat until melted, then
   pour over the oat mixture and stir until well
   combined. Stir in the salt, if using, and any
   other flavouring (see box).

5. Divide the mixture between the baking sheets.
   Cover with more baking parchment and roll
   the mixture out to an even layer, about 5
   mm/¼ inch thick. Remove the top layer of
   baking parchment (keep it for later) and, using
   the tip of a sharp knife, score the mixture into
   rectangles, about 10 on each tray.

6. Bake for 20–25 minutes, turning the sheets
   round halfway, until the crackers become
   golden around the edges, then turn them
   over. The easiest way to do this is to place
   the reserved baking parchment on top and –
   holding both sheets together carefully – flip
   them over.

7. Return the crackers to the oven for another
   20 minutes until light golden and crisp. Leave
   to cool and crisp up further, before breaking
   along the scored lines into individual crackers.

Five ways with popcorn

Popcorn is a great weekend treat that all the family can enjoy – ideally in front of a favourite film.

Basic popcorn recipe

serves 4 · **prep** 5 minutes · **cook** 5 minutes

75 g/2½ oz **popping corn**

Put the popping corn in a very large saucepan, cover with a lid and place it over a high heat.

Holding the lid, cook the popcorn for about 3–5 minutes until it begins to pop. It will pop repeatedly and then finally stop popping altogether. Shake the pan continuously throughout the process to keep it moving.

Turn off the heat and remove the lid from the pan to allow the popcorn to cool a little before adding the flavouring of your choice.

Cheesy popcorn

75 g/2½ oz **Parmesan cheese**, grated

1 quantity basic **popcorn** (above)

½ teaspoon **mild chilli powder** (optional)

Scatter the Parmesan in batches over the freshly cooked, warm popcorn, shaking the pan gently and stirring through each batch of cheese before adding the next. Keep going until all the popcorn is lightly covered and the cheese has melted a little.

Scatter over ½ teaspoon mild chilli powder (if using) before serving.

Bacon-flavoured popcorn

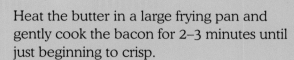

125 g/4½ oz **unsmoked back bacon**, finely shredded

1 quantity basic **popcorn** (opposite)

50 g/1¾ oz **unsalted butter**

Heat the butter in a large frying pan and gently cook the bacon for 2–3 minutes until just beginning to crisp.

Add the butter and bacon mixture to the cooked popcorn and toss until combined. Serve warm.

Caramel popcorn

50 g/1¾ oz **unsalted butter**

2 tablespoons **light muscovado sugar**

2 tablespoons **double cream**

1 quantity basic **popcorn** (opposite)

Melt the butter in a small saucepan, then add the sugar and stir well for about 2 minutes until it dissolves.

Remove the pan from the heat and add the cream, stirring well until a caramel has formed. Pour this over the freshly cooked popcorn and gently toss to lightly coat.

Peanut butter popcorn

25 g/1 oz **unsalted butter**

2 tablespoons **soft brown sugar**

3 tablespoons no-salt, no-sugar **smooth peanut butter**

1 quantity basic **popcorn** (opposite)

Heat the butter in a large saucepan, then add the sugar and stir well for about 2 minutes until it dissolves. Stir in the peanut butter.

Add the cooked popcorn to the peanut butter mixture in batches, tossing gently each batch to lightly coat.

Cinnamon popcorn

50 g/1¾ oz **unsalted butter**

2 tablespoons **demerara sugar**

½ teaspoon **ground cinnamon**

1 quantity basic **popcorn** (opposite)

Heat the butter in a small saucepan, then add the sugar and cinnamon and stir well for about 2 minutes until the sugar dissolves.

Pour the cinnamon mixture over the freshly made popcorn and gently toss to lightly coat.

Mix + match crumbly cookies

makes 20–24 · prep 30 minutes · cook 15 minutes
+ chilling

This cookie dough combination was made to inspire budding designers. From splats to plaits and from rocks to rolls, let imaginations go wild and little fingers get messy!

What you need

125 g/4½ oz **unsalted butter**

100 g/3½ oz **caster sugar**

1 teaspoon **vanilla extract**

1 **egg**

200 g/7 oz **plain flour**, plus extra for dusting

1 teaspoon **baking powder**

1 tablespoon **cocoa powder**

1 tablespoon finely grated **orange** zest

Cookie art

Rolling, squishing and cutting the cookie dough are cooking activities simply made for tiny hands. Get the kids involved all the way through with this one.

What to do

1. In a mixing bowl, cream together the butter, sugar and vanilla extract until light and fluffy. Beat in the egg. Sift in the flour and baking powder and stir to make a smooth, soft dough.

2. Split the dough in half and place one half in a separate mixing bowl. Add the cocoa powder to one half and stir in until completely chocolatey. Stir the orange zest into the other bowl of dough. Divide each type of dough into 4 equal pieces.

3. Generously flour a work surface. Roll each piece of dough into a sausage shape about 30 cm/12 inches long. Place 1 chocolate and 1 orange cylinder side by side and lightly press them together. Beginning at one end, turn the cylinders to create a spiral. Repeat to make 4 dough spirals.

4. Place on a baking tray lined with baking parchment and freeze for 10 minutes to firm up.

5. Preheat the oven to 180°C/350°F/Gas Mark 4. Line a second baking tray with baking parchment.

6. When chilled, flatten each wheel of dough with a rolling pin on a floured work surface, then use cookie cutters to cut 2-tone cookies. Place the cookies, spaced well apart, on the lined baking trays and bake for 12–15 minutes until light golden. Cool on a wire rack.

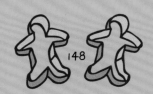

Awesome orange + ginger cake

makes
9
squares

prep
20 minutes

cook
40–45 minutes

This cake is a sweet and scrummy introduction to ginger – have fun helping your little ones discover new flavours for their developing taste buds.

What you need

175 g/6 oz **unsalted butter,** plus extra for greasing

150 g/5½ oz **golden syrup**

225 g/8 oz **self-raising flour**

2 teaspoons **ground ginger**

1 teaspoon **ground cinnamon**

190 g/6¾ oz **orange marmalade**

2 **eggs**, lightly beaten

2 tablespoons **whole milk**

What to do

1. Preheat the oven to 180°C/350°F/Gas Mark 4. Grease a 20 cm/8 inch square cake tin and line the base with baking parchment.

2. Melt the butter and syrup in a small saucepan over a low heat, stirring well to combine. Remove the mixture from the heat and set aside.

3. Sift the flour, ginger and cinnamon in a large mixing bowl, then slowly pour the syrup mixture into the bowl, stirring with a wooden spoon until combined. Beat the marmalade into the eggs and milk in a jug and stir into the cake mixture until the batter is smooth.

4. Pour the mixture into the cake tin, spreading it out evenly if necessary, and bake for 40–45 minutes until golden and firm to the touch. It is ready when a skewer inserted into the middle of the cake comes out clean.

5. Allow the cake to cool for 15 minutes in the tin before carefully removing it to a wire rack. Cut the cake into squares and serve warm or cold, with a spoonful of thick natural yogurt or a scoop of vanilla ice cream.

I might be a bit too hot for your pocket!

Pizza pocket bites

makes 8 · prep 20 minutes · cook 25 minutes + proving

These are no ordinary bread rolls – they're bite-sized and have pizza flavours buried in the centre to tantalise the taste buds. Eat them on their own or as an accompaniment to pasta dishes. For a veggie alternative, leave out the pepperoni.

What you need

2 x 145 g/5¼ oz packets **pizza-base mix**

2 tablespoons finely chopped **oregano**

A little **flour**, for dusting

1 tablespoon **olive oil**

¼ each small **red**, **yellow** and **green pepper**, deseeded and roughly sliced

50 g/1¾ oz **pepperoni**, roughly chopped

100 g/3½ oz **Cheddar cheese**, grated

What to do

1. Preheat the oven to 220°C/425°F/Gas Mark 7.

2. Put the pizza-base mix in a bowl with the oregano, add the required amount of warm water according to the packet instructions and mix thoroughly to form a smooth dough.

3. Turn the dough onto a lightly floured surface and knead until it is smooth.

4. Heat the oil in a heavy-based frying pan and cook the peppers over a moderate heat for 4–5 minutes until soft, then add the pepperoni and cook for a further minute.

5. Divide the dough into 8 equal pieces and make a well in the centre of each. Place equal amounts of the peppers and pepperoni in each well and very roughly knead them into the dough. Shape the dough pieces into balls and place them on a baking sheet. Cover with a damp cloth and leave to prove for 30 minutes, or until they have roughly doubled in size.

6. Sprinkle the balls with the Cheddar and bake them for 20 minutes until they are golden and cooked through – when they're cooked, the base of each pizza bite should sound hollow when you tap it. Serve the pizza bites while they are still warm.

Can I help?

Kneading time

Your toddler can help you to knead the veggies into the dough pieces and roll them into balls – brilliant foody play that helps to get the job done!

Flour dough fun

Our special cloud dough is so much fun – and, best of all, it's super-easy to make. It's also messy, so give everyone an apron and cover the table before you get started.

1

Mix it up

In a bowl mix together 8 cups of cornflour and 1–2 cups of vegetable oil. Work it all together to combine. Little fingers get stuck in straight away – getting messy is all part of the fun.

2

Add the sparkle

Add in a few sprinkles of glitter and mix them through. Now it's like fairy dust! The dough should hold together when gently moulded, but crumble away if you apply pressure.

3

Watch the magic

When the dough is all fully mixed, it's time to play. Put the cloud dough into a large tray, then mould it into shapes – a bit like building lots of sparkly sandcastles. When you're ready, knock them down and build some more!

Magic goop

When you've had enough of cloud dough, try magic goop instead. In a big bowl mix together 500 g/1 lb 2 oz cornflour and 2 cups of water. Add food colouring – the brighter the better, but be careful, as it may stain your clothes. Then watch! At first the goop feels quite firm, but suddenly it will stream through little fingers like magic. Make your goop sparkle by adding some twinkly glitter; or make it smell delicious with a drop or two of peppermint essence.

Cheesy straw dippers

We think these are the flakiest, cheesiest, most perfect cheese straws we've ever tasted. They taste even better when they're dunked in our cheesy pesto dip.

What you need

50 g/1¾ oz **unsalted butter**, softened, plus extra for greasing

250 g/9 oz **Cheddar cheese**, grated

125 g/4½ oz **wholemeal flour**, plus extra for dusting

1 **egg**, lightly beaten

2 tablespoons **sesame seeds**

¼ teaspoon **mild chilli powder** or **paprika**

For the pesto dip

2 tablespoons **pesto**

50 g/1¾ oz **cream cheese**

2 tablespoons **whole milk**

What to do

1. Preheat the oven to 200°C/400°F/Gas Mark 6.

2. In a food processor cream the butter and Cheddar. Stir in the flour and form the mixture into a soft dough.

3. On a lightly floured surface, roll out the dough until it is 1.5 cm/⅝ inch thick. Brush the flattened dough with the beaten egg, then cut it into 5 cm/2 inch strips. Sprinkle the strips with the sesame seeds and the chilli powder or paprika.

4. Put the strips on a lightly greased baking sheet and bake them for 10–15 minutes until crisp.

5. Meanwhile, make the dip by mixing the pesto with the cream cheese and the milk until fully combined. Place in a small dipping bowl and serve with the warm cheese straws.

Rollin' rollin' rollin'

Can I help?

Lightly flour your work surface, place your ball of cheesy dough on it and let your little helper roll away. Once the dough is flat, he or she can brush over the egg glaze, too.

Carroty cakes

makes 16 squares   prep 20 minutes   cook 30 minutes

Carrots make a wonderfully moist cake. These little treats are especially good because the decorations are made from real carrot shavings.

What you need

200 g/7 oz **carrots**

175 g/6 oz **soft brown sugar**

200 g/7 oz **self-raising flour**

1 teaspoon **bicarbonate of soda**

2 teaspoons **ground cinnamon**

Finely grated zest of 1 **orange**

2 **eggs**, beaten

150 ml/¼ pint **sunflower oil**

For the topping

50 g/1¾ oz **unsalted butter**, softened

75 g/2½ oz **icing sugar**

120 g/4¼ oz **cream cheese**

Carrot shavings, to decorate (optional)

What to do

1. Preheat the oven to 180°C/350°F/Gas Mark 4. Grease an 18 cm/7 inch square cake tin.

2. Grate the carrots finely into a large mixing bowl. Sift the sugar, flour, bicarbonate of soda and cinnamon on top of the carrot, then add the orange zest and mix everything together. Add the eggs and the oil to the mixture. Mix everything together well.

3. Spoon the mixture into the cake tin and level the top. Bake for 30 minutes or until the cake is cooked through – test it by piercing it with a metal skewer. It should come out clean. Remove the cake from the oven and leave it to cool in the tin placed on a wire rack.

4. Meanwhile, make the topping. Mix the butter and icing sugar together, then stir in the cream cheese until smooth.

5. When the cake is cool, carefully turn it out of the tin and onto a board. Spread the topping evenly over the cake and cut the cake into 16 squares. Decorate each square with a shaving of fresh carrot, if you wish.

❄ Freeze the cake and icing separately.

Everyone loves a lazy weekend breakfast —
especially if it occasionally turns into lunch!
Here are some tasty ideas for leisurely breakfasts
that little ones can get involved in making themselves —
with a little bit of supervision from the grown-ups.

Very berry smoothie

serves **4**   prep **5** minutes   ❄

Full of fruity goodness and great for slurping, this smoothie is always a hit.

75 g/2½ oz **vanilla yogurt**
175 g/6 oz **frozen berries** or **fresh fruit** (mango, pineapple, raspberries, or whatever is in season)
1 ripe **banana**
150 ml/¼ pint **whole milk**

Place all the ingredients in a food processor and whiz until smooth. Pour into 4 glasses and serve immediately.

❄ Pop this in the freezer and you will end up with ice cream!

What colour?

Before you whiz up the fruit, have a go at guessing what colour the smoothie is going to be. Talk about the colours of the individual fruits and then older toddlers can try to predict the result.

Purple pancakes

Who said pancakes have to be yellow? Squished blueberries added to the batter make pancakes that are purple – a special surprise for the weekend.

150 g/5½ oz **self-raising flour**

1 **egg**

150 ml/¼ pint **whole milk**

50 g/1¾ oz **blueberries**

Unsalted butter, for frying

Maple syrup, to serve (optional)

Fresh fruit, to serve (optional)

Sift the flour into a small mixing bowl and make a well in the centre.

Break the egg into a jug, add the milk, and mix well. Pour the mixture into the well and, using a balloon whisk, draw the flour into the liquid gradually and mix it all together until combined to a smooth batter.

Place the blueberries in a small bowl and, using a hand blender, whiz until almost smooth and very purple!

Pour the purple purée into the pancake batter and mix well.

Wipe the base of a large, heavy-based frying pan with a little butter and heat. Pour large spoonfuls of the batter, spaced well apart, into the the pan and cook the pancakes for about 1 minute, then flip them over using a fish slice and cook for 30–60 seconds more until golden brown on both sides.

Transfer the pancakes to a plate and keep them warm. Repeat the process until all the batter is used up. Serve the pancakes warm with a little maple syrup and fresh fruit (if using).

Scale school

Can I help?

Measuring out the blueberries is a good introduction for little ones to using scales – and less messy than measuring out flour or sugar!

Holey moley pancakes

This is a variation on pikelets, courtesy of Kim who runs our Making Friends team here at Ella's Kitchen. She loves to make them with her nieces and nephews when they come to stay. The little holes are the secret to a great pancake taste experience.

125 g/4½ oz **plain flour**

½ teaspoon **baking soda**

½ teaspoon **cream of tartar**

1 **egg**

1 tablespoon **sugar**

25 g/1 oz **unsalted butter**, melted, plus extra for frying

150 ml/¼ pint **whole milk**

Fresh fruit, to serve (optional)

Mix the flour with the baking powder and cream of tartar. In a separate bowl, whisk the egg and sugar, then stir in the melted butter. Then, alternately add small amounts of the flour mixture and the milk to the egg mixture until everything is combined to a thick batter.

Wipe the base of a large, heavy-based frying pan with a little butter and heat. Spoon in individual tablespoons of the batter to form small pancakes. Cook for about 1 minute until the bubbles have burst, then flip the pancakes over using a fish slice and cook for 30 seconds more until golden brown on both sides.

Transfer the pancakes to a plate and keep them warm. Repeat the process until all the batter is used up. Serve the pancakes warm with fresh fruit (if using).

Strawberry, banana + mango porridge

serves 4 · prep 10 minutes · cook 10 minutes

This deliciously fruity porridge is just about the perfect start to the day – a warming breakfast that the whole family will want to try!

1 large **banana**, roughly chopped

125 g/4½ oz **strawberries**, hulled and roughly chopped

½ **mango**, roughly chopped

1½ tablespoons **clear honey**

½ teaspoon **ground cinnamon**

600 ml/1 pint **whole milk**

150 g/5½ oz **porridge oats**

Place the fruit in a saucepan with the honey, cinnamon and 2 tablespoons of water. Bring to the boil, stirring gently to combine, and cook over a medium heat for 3–4 minutes until the fruit is soft and a toffee-like sauce has formed.

In a separate pan, bring the milk to the boil, stirring occasionally, then remove it from the heat and add the porridge oats. Stir well, then return the pan to a low heat, stirring continuously for 5–6 minutes until the porridge has thickened.

Stir half the fruit mixture through the porridge and mix well, then ladle the fruity porridge into warmed serving bowls and spoon over the remaining fruit.

Slowly, slowly stirring

Can I help?

Older children can help you stir the porridge slowly – but keep a very attentive eye on them the whole time. Talk about how the mixture changes from runny to thick.

5 ways

Five ways with eggs

Lazy weekend breakfasts are made for sharing. We love that the humble egg lets us rustle up so many tastes and textures.

Scrambled egg + avocado

serves 2–4 | prep 5 minutes | cook 5 minutes

4 **eggs**, beaten

Unsalted butter, for frying

4 tablespoons **crème fraîche**

1 small **avocado**, roughly chopped

¼ teaspoon **paprika**

Freshly ground **black pepper**

Place the eggs in a small, heavy-based saucepan with the butter and cook them over a low heat, stirring continuously, until they begin to scramble.

Remove the eggs from the heat, season with a little pepper, then add the crème fraîche. Return the mixture to the heat and cook, stirring continuously, until the egg is cooked through, but the mixture is still soft.

Remove the eggs from the heat, stir in the avocado and paprika and serve with wholemeal toast fingers.

Lemon soufflé cloud omelette

serves 2 | prep 5 minutes | cook 4 minutes

3 **eggs**, separated

Juice and finely grated zest of 1 **lemon**

1 tablespoon **caster sugar**

Unsalted butter, for frying

1 teaspoon **icing sugar**

Whisk the egg whites until stiff. In a separate bowl mix together the egg yolks, the lemon juice and zest and the sugar.

Heat the butter in a medium-sized frying pan. Fold the egg whites and yolk mixture together, then pour it all into the pan.

Cook the omelette over a gentle heat for 2–3 minutes on one side, then flip it over and cook the other side for about 30 seconds until both sides are just golden.

Turn the omelette out of the pan onto a warmed serving plate and sprinkle with icing sugar.

Red cheesy scramble

serves 4 prep 5 minutes cook 4 minutes

Unsalted butter, for frying

4 **eggs**

4 tablespoons **whole milk**

75 g/2½ oz **red Leicester cheese**, grated

Heat the butter in a small, heavy-based saucepan over a low heat.

Beat the eggs, milk and red Leicester with a wooden spoon, then pour into the pan.

Stir continuously over the heat for 3–4 minutes until the eggs are softly scrambled and cooked through, and the cheese has melted.

Serve on a slice of toasted wholemeal soda bread if liked.

Posh ham + eggs

serves 4 prep 5 minutes cook 5 minutes

4 **eggs**

2 **muffins**, halved and toasted

4 thick slices good-quality **ham**

4 tablespoons **hollandaise sauce**

To poach the eggs, bring a small saucepan of lightly salted water to the boil. Stir the water briskly to create a whirlpool and then crack the eggs into it, 1 or 2 at a time, and cook for 2–3 minutes. Remove the eggs from the pan using a slotted spoon and keep warm.

Lightly toast the muffins and place each toasted half on a warmed serving plate. Top with a slice of ham and a poached egg. Spoon 1 tablespoon of hollandaise sauce over each egg to serve.

Cinnamon eggy bread

serves 4 prep 5 minutes cook 2–3 minutes

2 **eggs**, beaten

100 ml/3½ fl oz **whole milk**

1 teaspoon **ground cinnamon**

4 slices **brioche**

Unsalted butter, for frying

4 teaspoons **demerara sugar**

Place the eggs in a small bowl with the milk and ½ teaspoon of the cinnamon and beat together. Dip the brioche slices into the milk mixture, allowing it to soak in a little. Melt the butter in a large, heavy-based frying pan, then cook the eggy bread over a high heat for 1–2 minutes on each side until lightly golden. Mix the demerara sugar with the remaining cinnamon and sprinkle over the eggy bread.

For a bit of a special treat, why not have a day dedicated to chocolate? Have fun experimenting with different combinations of fruit and chocolate, or have a go at making the best chocolate cake ever. There's nothing quite like the gooey, chocolatey mess that happens when you tuck in!

Warm chocolate pots

serves **4** · prep **5** minutes · cook **5** minutes

This is a yummy cross between chocolate mousse and warm chocolate pot and we dare anyone not to like it! It's ideal for chocolate moustaches.

100 g/3½ oz **dark chocolate**, broken up (or you could use 50 g/1¾ oz dark chocolate and 50 g/1¾ oz milk chocolate)

300 g/10½ oz **fromage frais**

1 teaspoon **vanilla extract**

cocoa powder, for dusting (optional)

Melt the chocolate in a bowl over a pan of gently simmering water. When the chocolate has melted, remove the pan from the heat.

Take the bowl off the pan and add the fromage frais and vanilla extract, quickly stirring it all together until the ingredients are fully combined.

Divide the chocolate mixture between 4 little pots, cups or glasses. Dust with cocoa powder (if using) and serve immediately.

Fruity fun choccie dippers

serves **6** · prep **5** minutes · cook **10** minutes

Delicious fruit pieces dunked in three kinds of runny chocolate – lip-smackingly good!

100 g/3½ oz **milk chocolate**, broken up

100 g/3½ oz **white chocolate**, broken up

100 g/3½ oz **dark chocolate**, broken up

Slices of **apple**, **pear**, **melon** and **pineapple**, halved **grapes** and whole **strawberries**, for dunking

Put the pieces of milk, white and dark chocolate into 3 separate bowls.

In turn, place each bowl over a pan of gently simmering water and melt the 3 types of chocolate until each becomes smooth, glossy and runny.

Transfer each type of chocolate into its own serving dish and serve immediately with bowls of the fruit on the side for dunking.

Best-ever chocolate cake

serves 10 | prep 20 minutes | cook 40-50 minutes

Whether it be for a birthday or other celebration, or a simple afternoon tea, every family needs a best-ever chocolate cake recipe. Listen for the chorus of 'More, please!'

150 g/5½ oz **plain flour**

50 g/1¾ oz good-quality **cocoa powder**

1 heaped teaspoon **baking powder**

175 g/6 oz **unsalted butter**, softened

150 g/5½ oz **light muscovado sugar**

3 **eggs**, beaten

250 ml/9 fl oz **soured cream**

1 tsp **vanilla essence**

For the icing

100 g/3½ oz **plain chocolate**, broken up

150 g/5½ oz **unsalted butter**, softened

125 g/4½ oz **cream cheese**

175 g/6 oz **icing sugar**, sifted

50 g/1¾ oz **milk**, **dark** and **white chocolate**, grated, to decorate

Preheat the oven to 180°C/350°F/Gas Mark 4. Grease a 20 cm/8 inch springform cake tin and line it with baking parchment.

Sift the flour, cocoa powder and baking powder into a bowl. In a separate bowl, cream together the butter and muscovado sugar until light and fluffy. A little at a time, add the beaten eggs with a spoonful of the flour mixture to the butter mixture, stirring continuously.

Add in the remaining flour mixture along with the soured cream and vanilla essence and fold everything together using a metal spoon. Pour the cake batter into the prepared tin and bake for 40–50 minutes until the cake has risen and is firm to the touch. The cake is ready when a skewer inserted into the centre comes out clean. Cool the cake in the tin for 20 minutes, then turn it out onto a wire rack to cool completely.

Meanwhile, make the icing. Melt the chocolate in a bowl set over a pan of gently simmering water. Once it has melted, set it aside to cool. In a separate bowl beat the butter and cream cheese with a wooden spoon until combined. Beat in the icing sugar, then the cooled chocolate, taking care not to overbeat.

Cut the cooked cake in half horizontally and use a third of the icing to sandwich the two pieces together. Transfer the cake to a serving board or plate and cover the top and sides with the remaining icing. Decorate with the grated chocolate.

Freeze the cake and icing separately.

The smell of homemade pizza baking in the oven is utterly delicious. Transforming your kitchen into a pizza café means there's plenty for everyone to do — from creating the menus and taking the orders to preparing the pizza dough and arranging the toppings. Have fun!

Potato pizza

100 g/3½ oz **plain flour**, plus extra for dusting

¼ teaspoon **fast-action dried yeast**

2 teaspoons **sugar**

75 g/2½ oz mashed **potato**

1 **egg**, beaten

5 tablespoons **pizza sauce** or **Clever Tomato Sauce** (see page 32)

6 **sunblush tomatoes**

75 g/2½ oz **mozzarella cheese**, grated

Basil leaves, to serve

In a small bowl, combine the flour, yeast and sugar. Add the mashed potato and mix. The dough should look clumpy. Add 3 tablespoons of water and then the egg and stir with a spatula until the mixture forms a loose dough.

Knead the dough on a lightly floured surface until it becomes smooth. Put it in a bowl, cover the bowl with a damp tea towel and set aside in a warm place to prove for 30 minutes.

Preheat the oven to 200°C/400°F/Gas Mark 6.

Knead the dough again on a lightly floured surface and roll it out to a circle measuring about 20 cm/8 inches in diameter. Place it on a large baking sheet, cover lightly with a tea towel and allow it to rest for a further 15 minutes. After this time, spread the dough with the pizza sauce or Clever Tomato Sauce, the tomatoes and mozzarella.

Bake the pizza for 20 minutes, until the mozzarella is bubbling and golden. Scatter basil leaves on top and serve the pizza cut into wedges. (Try some of the other topping suggestions on page 179, too.)

Roaring rocket pizza

serves **4** · prep **5** minutes · cook **8–10** minutes

This is the quickest pizza ever, and the rocket adds some greens. Children love the stringiness of the mozzarella.

- 4 small round **wholemeal pitta breads**
- 4 tablespoons **concentrated tomato purée** or **Clever Tomato Sauce** (see page 32)
- 125 g/4½ oz **mozzarella cheese**, cut into slices (or 4 handfuls of ready-grated mozzarella)
- 2 handfuls of **rocket** leaves

Preheat the oven to 220°C/425°F/Gas Mark 7.

Place the pitta breads on a baking sheet and spread each pitta evenly with the tomato purée or Clever Tomato Sauce, then cover each with mozzarella.

Bake the pizzas in the middle of the oven for 8–10 minutes, or until the cheese is melted and has turned golden brown.

Allow the cooked pizzas to cool for a few minutes, then sprinkle with rocket leaves and serve immediately.

Pesto pizza?

You can vary the toppings, and also the sauce. Instead of the purée or Clever Tomato Sauce, try spreading each pitta bread with 2 teaspoons of tomato pesto from a jar.

Colour me in

DIY pizza pie

Can I help?

Spreading over luscious helpings of tomato purée with a plastic knife, or with a butter knife that has a rounded end, is a great way for children to get involved. They can sprinkle over their own toppings, too.

Scone pizza

Pizzas don't have to be round. Use a cookie cutter to create your favourite shape. Choose your toppings. Adding herbs to the scone mixture in these pizzas makes for extra tastiness.

500 g/1 lb 2 oz **self-raising flour**
250 g/9 oz **ricotta cheese**
1 **egg**
3 tablespoons finely chopped mixed **fresh herbs** (such as basil, parsley and oregano)
4 **sun-dried tomatoes**, drained and roughly chopped
250 ml/9 fl oz **whole milk**
4 tablespoons **sun-dried tomato purée** or **Clever Tomato Sauce** (see page 32)
75 g/2½ oz **black olives**, pitted and roughly chopped
75 g/2½ oz **mozzarella cheese**, finely chopped
Freshly ground **black pepper**, to taste

Preheat the oven to 200°C/400°F/ Gas Mark 6.

Sift the flour into a food processor fitted with the plastic blade and season with a little freshly ground black pepper.

In a bowl, beat the ricotta, egg, herbs, tomatoes and milk together well. Add this cheese mixture to the flour in the food processor and beat to make a soft dough.

Turn out the dough onto a lightly floured surface. Roll it out to form a rough 23 cm/ 9 inch circle. (Cut your dough shapes now if you wish.) Place the dough circle or shapes on a baking sheet.

Spread the dough with the sun-dried tomato purée or Clever Tomato Sauce, scatter with the olives and sprinkle over the chopped mozzarella.

Bake for 25 minutes until the cheese is golden and bubbling.

Create your own

> Can I help?

Mini chefs will love to roll out the dough and then use their favourite shape cutters to make their own personalised pizzas. They can help with the cheese sprinkling, too.

Toppings to try

- Peppers
- Ham
- Mushrooms
- Grated courgette
- Fresh pineapple
- Cooked, sliced aubergine
- Sun-dried tomatoes
- Canned tuna
- Cooked prawns
- Cooked chicken (try some teriyaki chicken)
- No-salt, no-sugar sweetcorn
- Olives
- Cooked egg
- Cooked sausage
- Chocolate + banana

The sight, sound and smell of food sizzling on the BBQ
is one of summer's great delights. Children will love to be
involved in the grilling process, with careful supervision.
Little hands also make light work of kebab preparations,
wrapping food in foil parcels, and mixing salads and sauces.

Inside-out burgers

makes **8**   prep **15** minutes   cook **5** minutes

500 g/1 lb 2 oz **lean minced beef**

3 tablespoons finely chopped **flat-leaf parsley**

1 tablespoon **wholegrain mustard**

125 g/4½ oz **Gruyère cheese**, cut into 8 small equal slices

8 small **wholemeal burger buns**, to serve

Rocket leaves and **tomato** slices, to serve

Freshly ground **black pepper**

Place the minced beef in a bowl, add the parsley and mustard, season well with plenty of freshly ground black pepper, and mix well with a fork.

Divide the mixture into 8 equal pieces. Break each piece in half and shape each half into a thin patty. Top one of the patties with a slice of Gruyère (the cheese should sit within the patty with at least a 1 cm/½ inch border around it – shape the meat into a larger patty, if necessary). Place the other patty over the top and press around the edges to secure the cheese inside. Prepare the rest of the burgers in the same way.

Cook the burgers on a wire rack over the hot coals for 4–5 minutes on each side until coloured and cooked through.

Serve the burgers in wholemeal buns with rocket leaves and tomato slices.

❄ If freezing, do so before the burgers are cooked.

Sticky sausages

serves 4–6 | prep 5 minutes | cook 10–12 minutes

12 good-quality **chipolata sausages**

1 tablespoon **olive oil**

For the glaze

3 tablespoons **clear honey**

2 tablespoons **wholegrain mustard**

2 tablespoons finely chopped **flat-leaf parsley**

Freshly ground **black pepper**

Place the sausages on a wire rack over the hot coals and cook them for 10–12 minutes, turning them until they are browned all over and cooked through. Remove the sausages from the heat and cut each one in half.

Place the honey, wholegrain mustard and parsley in a large bowl and mix well, seasoning with a little freshly ground black pepper. Add the hot sausages to the bowl and toss them to coat with the glaze.

Serve the coated sausages in a bowl and give everyone cocktail sticks or small forks to prevent sticky fingers. They are delicious accompanied with sticks of carrot, red pepper and celery.

Buttery corn on the cob

serves 4 | prep 5 minutes | cook 12 minutes

4 cobs fresh **sweetcorn**

50 g/1¾ oz **unsalted butter**, slightly softened

1 teaspoon **paprika**

1 tablespoon finely chopped **flat-leaf parsley**

Cut each cob in half. Bring a large saucepan of lightly salted water to the boil and blanch the cobs for 5 minutes. Remove them from the pan.

Cook the blanched cobs on a wire rack over the hot coals for 6–7 minutes until they are lightly charred and tender.

Meanwhile, place the butter in a small mixing bowl with the paprika and parsley and mix well. Place the cobs on serving plates and divide 'knobs' of the flavoured butter between them, allowing it to melt all over. Serve immediately.

182

Crunchy veggie kebabs

serves **4** prep **10** minutes cook **5–6** minutes

1 **courgette**, halved lengthways and cut into chunks

1 small **orange pepper**, deseeded and cut into chunks

1 small **red pepper**, deseeded and cut into chunks

8 **chestnut mushrooms**, halved

2 tablespoons **olive oil**

For the glaze

1 tablespoon **tomato ketchup** or **Clever Tomato Sauce** (see page 32)

1 tablespoon **clear honey**

1 teaspoon **Dijon mustard**

Divide the prepared vegetables evenly between 8 well-soaked bamboo skewers or 8 metal skewers, threading them on in a repeating pattern. Lightly brush each kebab with the oil.

Cook the kebabs on a wire rack over the hot coals for 5–6 minutes, turning occasionally, until the vegetables are lightly charred in places and tender.

Meanwhile make the glaze. Mix together the tomato ketchup or Clever Tomato Sauce, the honey and mustard.

Remove the kebabs from the heat and lightly brush them with the glaze.

Banana chocolate treasure

4 ripe **bananas**

4–8 teaspoons **golden syrup**

100 g/3½ oz **plain chocolate**, roughly chopped

½ teaspoon **ground cinnamon**

Vanilla ice cream, to serve (optional)

Slit each banana in half along its length. Place each banana half on a piece of aluminium foil large enough to wrap it up.

Before you wrap, drizzle each length of banana with a teaspoon of the golden syrup, then sprinkle each with a little of the chopped chocolate. Finish with a sprinkle of the cinnamon.

Wrap the bananas, scrunching up the foil and leaving a small air pocket at the top of each parcel to let out the steam.

Place the foil-wrapped bananas on a wire rack over the hot coals and cook for 10–12 minutes until the bananas are soft and the sauce is hot.

Serve with a spoonful of vanilla ice cream (if using).

Fruity mallow kebabs

serves **4** prep **10 minutes** cook **1 minute**

1 slightly underripe **banana**, cut into chunks

8 **strawberries**, hulled

½ firm **mango**, stoned and cut into chunks

8 **marshmallows**

½ teaspoon **ground cinnamon**

Divide the fruit and marshmallows between 4 soaked bamboo skewers or 4 metal skewers.

Place the kebabs on a wire rack over the hot coals and cook for 20–30 seconds on each side until the marshmallows start to go soft and gooey (don't leave them too long or they will melt completely).

Sprinkle the cinnamon over the kebabs and serve immediately, while the marshmallows are still soft.

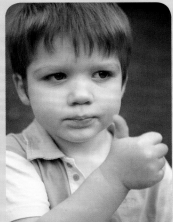

Index

Thank you

A big thank you to all of the
Ella's Kitchen employees and
friends who contributed recipes
for this book and 'road-tested'
them with their own families.

A special thank you to all our little
helpers – and their parents and
carers – for their patience in front
of the camera. Here's a list of our
little stars and their ages on the days
of our photo shoots:

Adam Bennett (age 3)
Alexander Rogoff (age 3)
Amélie Fricker (age 4)
Amélie Holladay (age 3)
Anna Thomas (age 3)
Annabelle Wilson (age 5)
Ava Di Palma (age 2)
Bella Douglas (age 2)
Ben Fleming (age 2)
Bruce Feng (age 5)
Callum McDonnell (age 1)
Carys Davies (age 3)
Charlie Douglas (age 4)

Charlie Newman (age 18 months)
Chloe Dale (age 3)
Conor Rennard (age 2)
Daisy Hawke (age 2)
Dan Heskia (age 5)
Daniel Woods (age 2)
Dhruv Reddi (age 2)
Dylan Standen (age 2)
Elodie Ramus (age 18 months)
Emily Preddy (age 3)
Emma Clements (age 3)
Ethan Wilson (age 7)
Finley Mason (age 19 months)
Florence Partridge (age 20 months)
George Hawke (age 4)
Harrison Slaughter (age 2)
Jackson Brooks-Dutton (age 2)
Jessica Brahams (age 3)
Keeley Carson (age 2)
Marnie Clew (age 2)
Michaela Bruce (age 4)
Millie Roxburgh (age 4)
Noah Quinn (age 3)
Olivia O'Brien (age 4)
Olivia Thaw (age 3)
Ollie Woodall (age 3)

Otis Lindsay (age 3)
Parisa A Sadique (age 2)
Poppy Kelly (age 1)
Poppy Nightingale (age 2)
Rosie Beverley (age 2)
Sam Hullis (age 4)
Sebastian Chippindale-Vives (age 2)
Sofia Walker (age 2)
Theo Hendry (age 2)
Tom Crickmay Rack (age 2)
Tyler Thaw (age 4)
Xanthe Grayburn (age 2)

For letting us take photos at their
homes, for providing recipe
inspiration and all of the other
important stuff that was needed to
make our very first cook book:

Vanessa Bird, Michelle Bowen,
Lee Faber, Nicki Harrold,
Catherine Hullis, Alison Lindley,
Anita Mangan, Lisa Mangan,
Mikha Mekler, Jane Middleton,
Victoria Millar

Stickers!

Stars and hearts for the recipes you love and more to decorate your pages!